MINI

MALLORCA

How to download your Free eBook

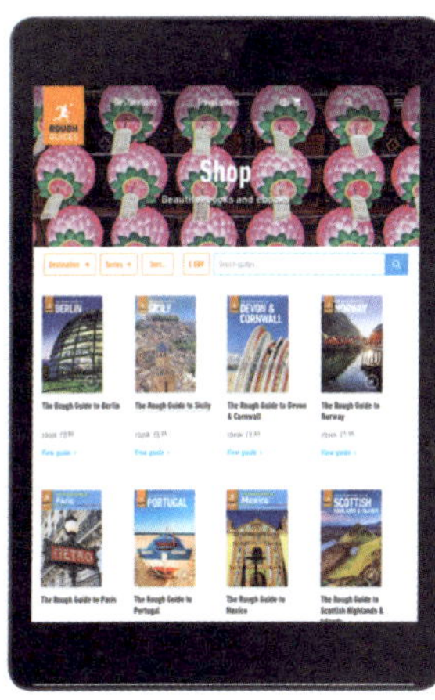

1. Visit **www.roughguides.com/free-ebook** or scan the **QR code** opposite
2. Enter the code **mallorca093**
3. Follow the simple step-by-step instructions

For troubleshooting contact: mail@roughguides.com

Samsonite

Contents

Introduction

Mallorca could claim to be the perfect holiday island, blessed with attributes that entice millions of foreign visitors annually. The deep blue and translucent turquoise of the Mediterranean, hundreds of kilometres of coastline, secluded rocky coves and wide sandy beaches, a vibrant and sophisticated capital city and some three hundred days of brilliant sunshine each year make it irresistible.

A varied landscape

Lying off the northeast coast of Spain, Mallorca is the largest of the five Balearic Islands, but it is not a big place. It has more than 550km (325 miles) of coastline, but at its widest point – Cap de Sa Mola in the southwest to Capdepera in the northeast – it is only 100km (60 miles) across; at its narrowest, from the Badia d'Alcúdia in the north to the Badia de Palma in the south, it's only half that distance.

The landscape, however, is extremely varied. The dramatic cliffs edging the Serra de Tramuntana, a World Heritage Site, hug the west coast from Andratx all the way to Cap de Formentor. The coastal scenery is stunning, with dizzying drops to the sea and the tiny coves far below and picturesque villages set among centuries-old terraces. To the northwest, away from the coast, the Tramuntana range provides ideal walking and climbing conditions. There are ten main peaks, the highest of which is Puig Major at 1,445 metres (4,741ft). The north coast is dominated by the Bay of Alcúdia – 12km (8 miles) of

NOTES

Mallorca's beaches didn't always have the sterling reputation they do today. Following a major clean-up campaign, 21 of the 32 Blue Flag beaches in the Balearic Islands belong to Mallorca, a testament to their safety and cleanliness.

fine golden sand sloping into shallow waters – and by the grassy wetlands of S'Albufera, now a protected natural park. The interior is a large plain with sleepy towns, sandstone churches, well-tended farmland, groves of ancient olive trees, vineyards and orchards of almonds and apricots.

Views along the west coast

On the east coast, long sweeps of beach give way to intimate little coves and spectacular cave formations, while several picturesque fishing harbours retain their individuality. The south centres on the cosmopolitan capital, Palma, and its splendid bay. Around it, to the east and west, spread the crowded beaches whose glorious sands first lured mass tourism to the island in the late 1950s.

Balmy climate

Mallorca's climate is heavenly for northern Europeans. Although summer extremes of 34°C (93°F) can be uncomfortable, the July and August average is a balmy 24°C (76°F); winters are mild and not too wet, and even the timid can swim in the sea from June to October.

Bougainvillea and birdlife

The flora of the island is as diverse as the landscape. There are cultivated olives, almonds, apricot and citrus trees; holm oaks and pines flourish in mountainous regions, with rosemary, lavender and heather turning the hillsides purple. Sturdy palm trees grow at sea level, and bougainvillea brightens village walls; while wild orchids and water-loving reeds, sedges and poplars thrive in the S'Albufera marshes.

Mallorca is rich in birdlife. Visit in spring, as so many birdwatchers do, to glimpse the numerous migratory birds that set up temporary home here. The Boquer Valley, near Pollença, is popular with those in the know. S'Albufera, on the north coast, plays host to resident and migrant species, including the cattle egrets that can be seen perched on the backs of cows, pecking insects from their hides, and birds of prey such as Eleonora's falcons, which typically

Magaluf was among the first of the large-scale resorts

WHEN TO GO

There's never a bad time to visit Mallorca, although the temperatures and crowds of the summer months can be tiring and relentless. That said, all the resorts and hotels are open during the peak season, offering visitors the full range of options that are often not available in winter. Spring and autumn can be prime times to land on the island as the weather is still sunny and the temperatures are generally warm but more comfortable for hiking and strenuous pursuits, plus you won't have to compete with crowds. If you're cost-conscious, out-of-season prices are generally lower. Look out for festivals and events throughout the year, though, when crowds swell and prices skyrocket, such as the Ta-Palma food festival in November or the Half Marathon Magaluf every April.

arrive in late spring and hang around until late October to early November. Among the most colourful and exotic species that can be seen in summer are bee-eaters and hoopoes. The island of Cabrera and the Parc Natural de Mondragó in the southeast corner are the best places to spot migrating seabirds.

The islanders

The population of Mallorca is approximately 966,000, of whom around half – 486,000 – live in the capital. The rest are scattered across 53 municipal districts, with the interior plain – Es Pla – being the most sparsely populated region. In the peak summer season, tourists – some fifteen million a year, a large proportion of whom are German or English – and hordes of seasonal workers, many from Andalucía, swell the population and strain the infrastructure and water supply to their limits.

Mallorcans are bilingual in Spanish and in Mallorquín, a variant of Catalan, which is the official language. Most signs and street names are written in Catalan, and this is the language people choose to speak among themselves, and which is used in schools. However, visitors will find locals quite happy to address them in Castilian Spanish, and the high number of seasonal workers from the mainland ensures that Spanish is spoken everywhere.

Tourism trends

Mallorca was one of the first places in Spain to be developed for tourism in the 1950s. Ever since, it has remained one of the major centres, and tourism is now responsible for nearly half of the island's income. But the industry has had contradictory effects. Income from it made this region Spain's wealthiest per capita, but the environmental effects of being Europe's low-budget playground have taken a heavy toll. Four decades after the initial explosion, tourism overheated, leaving a forest of towering hotels and beach-hugging villas, whole resorts lined with fast-food outlets and loud clubs and bars serving ludicrously cheap alcohol. This has led local residents to seek ways to limit so-called 'bad tourist

WHAT'S NEW

Over the past few years, Mallorca has revitalized its food and drink scene. Where once international buffets ruled, there is now a wealth of bars and restaurants championing locally sourced ingredients and creating dishes that are distinctly Mallorquí thanks to chefs such as Maca de Castro. From the high-end tasting menus of *Guethary* (see page 120) and *Voro* (www.vororestaurant.com) to market stalls like *Mercat Negre* (Plaça de l'Olivar) and shoreside dining at *El Chaval Beach Club* (www.elchavalmallorca.com), the island is shining a light on its standout produce from the sea and land. There's also been huge investment in top-tier accommodation, with global big-hitters like *Four Seasons* and *Mandarin Oriental* launching properties alongside Mallorca's own *Iberostar* brand, plus a wave of boutique and rural openings such as *Finca Banyols* (www.fincabanyols.com), *Castell Son Claret* (www.castellsonclaret.com) and *Cas Català* (www.cascatala.es).

activity', including changing how free alcohol is served at all-inclusive resorts and increasing the Sustainable Tourist Tax.

Puig de Randa monastery

In the 1990s, the island government realized it was time to reassess Mallorca's tourism industry. Fearing that massive overdevelopment and the increasingly bad reputation earned by the raucous behaviour of some visitors, as well as new trends in international tourism, were leaving the Balearics behind, the authorities took action. Moves to protect the remaining undeveloped areas included the creation of nature preserves, proclaiming them off-limits to construction, and demolishing some of the more unsightly hotel complexes. Almost one-third of the island is now under some kind of protection order, and the advantages to the landscape and wildlife are palpable.

There have also been energetic moves to encourage a more upmarket and environmentally friendly kind of tourism. The government's *agroturisme* initiative, which promotes accommodation in small rural hotels and *fincas* (farmhouses), has been extremely popular, both with visitors looking for peace and quiet amid scenic surroundings, and farming families who were struggling to keep their properties going.

Walking paths have been opened up and clearly marked, and a number of hilltop sanctuaries provide rest and respite for hikers;

natural parks are widely promoted and user-friendly. Considerable investment has been pumped into golf courses and marinas to attract higher-income tourists, and luxury resorts and boutique hotels are springing up all over the island.

In Palma de Mallorca, guided walking tours encourage visitors to appreciate the city's heritage, while the range and calibre of the capital's museums and cultural centres is impressive.

Enjoying the island

Throughout the island, summer music festivals are held in beautiful historic buildings, attracting internationally known performers, while traditional, local festivals are also being promoted as a way

Cala Ratjada

SUSTAINABLE TRAVEL

The Balearic Islands and in particular Mallorca have been a leader in trying to curb the negative effects of overtourism and promoting more sustainable travel. Visitors should be mindful about water use and waste, as water is a scarce resource. While car is still the easiest way to get around, consider buses, trains and tram services, which serve most of the island. While many people visit Mallorca to test their mettle cycling on the mountain roads, most of the major resorts are flat and jumping on a bike is a good and clean way to explore. Make sure to visit farmers' markets and the many agricultural businesses that support the local economy such as the salt plains of Salinas d'Es Trenc (see page 115) and vineyards of Binissalem (see page 79). Travelling out of the peak summer season is a great way to bolster the island year-round while helping to avoid overtourism particularly in popular beauty spots and sights.

of disseminating the rural culture of the Balearics. There has also been a renewed interest in Mallorcan food, *cuina Mallorquina*, and many venues, from the traditional *cellers* (see page 81) to gourmet restaurants are experiencing a surge in popularity.

Mallorca is easy to get around. Hiring a car is relatively inexpensive, but far from stress-free: many roads (especially the stretch around the Bay of Palma) get very busy, particularly in summer, and parking almost everywhere is a major pain. Public transport, however, is excellent: regular buses from Palma run to most points of interest (some services are limited on Sundays), and frequent rail services traverse the island – including the scenic journey on the narrow-gauge line between Palma and Sóller (see page 60). Alternatively, you can take to the water for scenic boat trips along the coast.

With all of this going for it, Mallorca is much more than simply a place for sun, sea and sand, though this holiday holy grail still rules the local roost.

10 Things not to miss

1

2

3

4

5

6

1 **VALLDEMOSSA**
One of the island's most enchanting inland towns. See page 54.

2 **BEACHES**
The island's pristine beaches, lapped by clear waters, are the biggest attraction for many visitors. See page 10.

3 **MONESTIR DE LLUC**
Wonderful views and soul-stirring singing at Mallorca's holiest site. See page 67.

4 **COVES DEL DRAC**
Beautifully presented caves, with one of the world's largest subterranean lakes. See page 86.

5 **DEIÀ**
Formerly the home of Robert Graves, and still one of the prettiest villages on the island. See page 58.

6 **FUNDACIÓ PILAR I JOAN MIRÓ**
Experience the life and work of one of Spain's most famous artists. See page 47.

7 **CAN PRUNERA**
Learn about *Modernisme* in this museum in Sóller. See page 60.

8 **SERRA DE TRAMUNTANA**
Stunning walks in a UNESCO-protected mountain range. See page 51.

9 **SINEU MARKET**
This traditional Wednesday-morning farmers' market is arguably the island's best. See page 79.

10 **PALMA'S CATHEDRAL**
Dominating the city and the harbour, this marvellous Gothic cathedral is a sight to behold. See page 35.

A perfect day in Mallorca

9AM

Breakfast. Kick off the day in Palma with breakfast at the trendy *Mise En Place* in Plaça Major, where a delicious array of treats – home-made pastries, cooked breakfasts, fruit pots – awaits. It's slightly hidden, but well worth seeking out.

10AM

In search of Chopin. Take the road that runs about 10km (6 miles) through olive and almond groves to Valldemossa, where La Real Cartuja holds the apartment in which George Sand and Frédéric Chopin once stayed. In Palau del Rei Sancho next door, recitals of Chopin's music are performed throughout the day.

NOON

Sweet treat. Linger over coffee and a *coca de patata*, a local pastry, in the Carrer Blanquerna.

1PM

Delightful Deià. Continue along the scenic coast road to Deià, a dinky, honey-coloured town that was home to poet Robert Graves and still attracts writers and artists. Meander through the picturesque streets and browse in the boutiques.

2PM

Graves's grave. Break for tapas in *El Barrigon Xelini* (see page 121), a huge, atmospheric bar with tables spilling outside onto a pleasant terrace. After, follow the literary trail and visit the poet's grave in the hilltop cemetery, before swinging by his home, Ca N'Alluny, which has been reimagined as a small museum.

3.30PM

Sea swims. Strike out on the 35-minute walk through olive and lemon groves to the Cala Deià, a pretty little rocky cove where you can swim in crystalline waters.

4.30PM

Sóller. From Deià, drive the wending coast road, flanked by orchards of citrus trees and gnarled olive groves, until you dip into the broad valley of Sóller. Explore the bustling little town itself, lined with well-preserved eighteenth- and nineteenth-century mansions. Pause for a coffee in the café-lined square, Plaça Sa Constitució, while admiring the *Moderniste* architecture and soaking up everyday local life.

6PM

Sunset. Head back down the coast to Son Marroig, home to a nineteenth-century Austrian archduke who fell in love with the island. You can visit his house and gardens, but the main attraction is sunset-gazing over Na Foradada.

8PM

Dinner. Take your pick from Deià's many fine restaurants. Go upmarket at *El Olivo* (part of *Belmond La Residencia*), or indulge in lobster with asparagus ravioli at *Sebastian* (see page 121).

Foodie Mallorca

9.30AM

Perfect pastries. Start your day at *Fornet de la Soca* (https://fornetdelasoca.com) in the Plaça de Weyler in Palma. This now-legendary bakery housed in the old Forn des Teatre makes some of the best pastries on the island. The owners have researched old recipes, and they use ancient Mallorcan flour grains. The queue is worth it.

9.45AM

Coffee time. Baked goods in hand, head up the nearby alleyway and step to *Mistral Coffee Banc* (https://mistralcoffee.com), Mallorca's first speciality coffee roaster for a takeaway *cortado*, then continue – cup and breakfast in tow – to the pretty Plaça Major and feel the city come to life.

10.30AM

Make for the market. Time for a spot of shopping, so leave the square and wander the busy shopping street of Carrer Sant Miquel until you reach the Basílica de Sant Miquel de Palma, then turn right to end up at the Mercat de l'Olivar (see page 43) – the city's main provisions market.

11AM

Stock up. Meander through the aisles of the market, taking in the sights, sounds and smells. Locals come here to shop for fresh fish, meat, fruit and vegetables, but you'll also find stalls selling spices, salt and more. Plenty of ideas for food souvenirs.

NOON

A light bite. Grab an early lunch at *Mercat Negre*, a corner stall where the team rustle up creative dishes in their tiny kitchen using fresh seafood from the market. Trust their judgement when it comes to ordering and perhaps pair your meal with a local wine.

1.30PM

Wine and vine. Talking of local wine, jump in a rental car and make your way on the Ma13 to *Bodega Ribas* (https://bodegaribas.com). This is the oldest winery in Mallorca, founded in 1711 and now run by the tenth generation of the family. Book in advance for a two-hour tour and tasting to learn about local grape varieties.

4.30PM

Get salty. Make tracks southeast to catch the last tour of the day at Salinas d'Es Trenc (book ahead; see page 115), which has been harvesting sea salt on these pans since the 1950s and the prized Flor de Sal is a hit with top chefs.

7PM

Sunset dinner. Drive ten minutes towards the coastal area of Colònia de Sant Jordi (see page 91) and linger over a sunset dinner at *Salivent* (see page 124). Its name means 'salt and wind' and the Mediterranean menu puts Mallorcan produce – including Flor de Sal – at the heart of its dishes.

Beach-hopping in Mallorca

9AM

Start the day. Wake up with an energetic dip in the shallow waters of Platja de Muro (see page 77), taking in the serene views of the Bay of Alcúdia and the backdrop of the Parc Natural de S'Albufera. Head to Port d'Alcúdia (see page 76) for a *café con leche* and tostada at *Ca Na Marcè* (https://canamarce.com); try to nab a table on the outdoor terrace.

11AM

Revealing ravine. Drive the winding mountain roads of the Ma10 into the Serra de Tramuntana towards Sa Colobra, a tiny cove with crystalline waters. Walk the coastal path through the manmade rock tunnel to the secluded mouth of the Torrent de Pareis (see page 66) river gorge, where a deep chasm widens into a huge natural amphitheatre.

1PM

Lunch in style. Jump back in the car and continue following the coast on the Ma10 until you reach the handsome seaside resort of Port de Sóller (see page 61), where you can grab a fresh fish lunch overlooking the sea at *Ses Oliveres* (Passeig Es Traves 18; https://sesoliveresportdesoller.com). Take a snap of the historic tram as it trundles past on its way to Sóller town.

3.30PM

Sunny afternoon. Drive through the mountains on the Ma11 and Ma1 to the southwest, where you can take a refreshing dip in the tiny cove of Portals Vells (see page 50) – often voted one of the best beaches in Mallorca – or try Platja del Mago if it's a bit crowded. Alternatively, stop in Magaluf for a drink at *El Chaval Beach Club* (Carrer Violetes 2; see page 121) and take a promenade stroll – the whole beachfront has undergone massive redevelopment over the past few years. Pick up picnic provisions at a local supermarket.

5.30PM

Sunset and seascapes. Follow the Ma1, Ma20 and Ma19 towards Es Trenc (see page 90). With more than 3km of powdery white sand and backed by natural protected wetlands, this beach is one of the most unspoiled on the island and is the best place to catch the sunset as you feast on your picnic – perhaps after a dusky swim.

History

Many influences have shaped Mallorca over the past four thousand years and helped make it the fascinating place it is today. The stone towers called *talayots* that still stud the island today were defensive structures built by early inhabitants, who are believed to have made settlements here around 1300BC. Even before that, Neolithic islanders had graduated from cave dwellings to simple stone houses, and cleared fields by piling stones into dividing walls – the origins of the intricate dry-stone walls called *parets seques* or *margers* still thread the island's interior.

Over the centuries, the inhabitants traded with the Phoenicians, Carthaginians and Greeks, and the Carthaginians gradually colonized the islands (c. 400BC), absorbed them into their trading empire and founded the main ports. But by 123BC, the Romans, who had pacified most of Spain, despatched an invading force to conquer the islands, which they named Balearis Major (Mallorca) and Balearis Minor (Menorca).

NOTES

The early inhabitants' skill with stones was evident in their deadly use of the slingshot. The 'Balearic slingers' were renowned throughout the Mediterranean world and recruited by Hannibal to fight for the Carthaginians in the Punic Wars against Rome. The name Balearic probably comes from the Greek word, *ballein*, 'to throw'.

Romans, vandals and Moorish occupation

The Romans introduced Christianity, built roads and established the towns of Palmaria (Palma) and Pollentia (near Alcúdia), but during the fifth century AD, as the Roman Empire crumbled, Goths, Vandals and Visigoths poured into the Balearics. The Vandals destroyed almost all

The talayotic settlement at Ses Païsses

evidence of Roman occupation – the remains of Pollentia outside Alcúdia are among the very few traces left – before they were ousted in 533AD by a Byzantine expedition from Constantinople.

But more invaders were hot on their heels. Ignited by the teachings of the Prophet Mohammed, Islam spread quickly in the eighth century. A Moorish army led by General Tarik landed on the Iberian Peninsula in 711 and in just seven years, most of Spain was under Moorish rule. While the Balearics remained submissive, the *caliphs* (rulers) were content to accept tribute from them, but local disturbances prompted an invasion at the beginning of the tenth century. Both islands were conquered and became part of the Caliphate of Córdoba.

Although little Moorish architecture remains – the Banys Àrabs in Palma and the Jardins d'Alfàbia near Sóller are two exceptions

– the influence can be seen in Palma, in the Palau de l'Almudaina, the fountains in S'Hort del Rei and in many shady patios. Some place names are also of Arabic origin – Alcúdia (Al-Kudia) means 'on the hill', and Binissalem 'son of peace'.

The reconquest

The aim of the crusades in Spain was the eviction of the Muslims or Moors – a process called the *reconquista*. In 1229, a Catalan army helmed by King Jaume I of Aragón and Catalunya seized Mallorca. Jaume proved to be an enlightened ruler who profited from the talents of the Moors – those who remained were forcibly converted to Christianity – as well as those of the large Jewish and Genoese trading communities.

The Banys Àrabs in Palma

Jaume I reigned in Aragón for six decades, but he made the mistake of dividing between his sons the lands he had united. Initially, this resulted in the Independent Kingdom of Mallorca, first under Jaume II, then under Sancho and Jaume III. But dynastic rivalry triggered the overthrow of the latter by his cousin, Pedro IV. Attempting to make a comeback, Jaume III was killed in battle near Llucmajor in 1349.

In the following century, the Catholic Monarchs, Ferdinand and Isabella, leading a unified Spain, completed the reconquest on the Spanish mainland, taking Granada, the only Moorish enclave left on the peninsula, in 1492.

The Spanish Empire

As one tumultuous age ended, another began. Christopher Columbus (Cristobal Colón), the seafaring captain from Genoa (whom at least three Mallorcan towns claim as their own), believed he could reach the East Indies by sailing westwards. In the same year that Granada fell, Columbus crossed the Atlantic. Spain exported its adventurers, traders and priests, and imposed its language, culture and religion on the New World, creating a vast empire in the Americas. Ruthless, avaricious conquistadors extracted and sent back incalculable riches in the form of silver and gold. The century and a half after 1492 was known as Spain's Golden Age, but it carried the seeds of its own decline. Plagued by corruption and incompetence, and drained of manpower and ships by such adventurism as the dispatch of the ill-fated *Armada* against England in 1588, Spain was unable to defend her expansive interests.

The Balearic Islands did not benefit much from Spain's glory years. They were forbidden to trade with the Americas, and their existing trade on the eastern routes was interrupted by marauding pirates based in North Africa, as well as by the powerful Turkish fleet.

Wars and consequences

The daughter of Ferdinand and Isabella married the heir to the Holy Roman Emperor, Maximilian of Habsburg. The Spanish crown duly passed to the Habsburgs and remained in their hands until the feeble-minded Carlos II died in 1700, leaving no heir. France seized the chance to install the young grandson of Louis XIV on the Spanish throne. A rival Habsburg claimant was supported by Austria and Britain, who saw a powerful Spanish–French alliance as a major threat. In the subsequent War of the Spanish Succession (1702–13), most of the kingdom of Aragón, including the Balearics, backed the Habsburgs. Britain seized Menorca and retained it, under the Treaty of Utrecht, when the war was over.

By 1805, Spain was once more aligned with France, and Spanish ships fought alongside the French against Admiral Lord Nelson at the Battle of Trafalgar. But Napoleon came to distrust his Spanish ally and forcibly replaced the king of Spain with his own brother, Joseph Bonaparte. A French army marched in to subdue the country. The Spanish resisted and aided by British troops, commanded by the Duke of Wellington, drove the French out. What the British call the Peninsular War (1808–14) is known in Spain as the War of Independence.

During the nineteenth century, most of Spain's possessions in the Americas broke away. The Balearics, further neglected, were beset with poverty, and thousands of islanders emigrated to South America in search of a better life. A brief upturn, due to the successful trade in wine, ended when the phylloxera louse destroyed the island's vines.

Crises, republic and Civil War

The beginning of the twentieth century in Spain was marked by social and political crises, assassinations and near anarchy. The colonial war in Morocco provided a distraction, but a disastrous defeat there in 1921 led to a coup and the dictatorship of General Primo de Rivera. He fell in 1929, and when elections of 1931 revealed massive anti-royalist feeling, the king followed him into exile.

The new republic was conceived amid an outbreak of strikes and uprisings. In February 1936, the left-wing Popular Front won a majority of seats in the Cortes (parliament), but across Spain, localized violence displaced debate. In July 1936, General Francisco Franco staged a coup, which was supported by key military regiments, monarchists, conservatives, the clergy and the right-wing Falangist movement. Aligned on the Republican government's side were liberals, socialists, communists and anarchists. The ensuing Spanish Civil War (1936–39) was brutal and bitter. Support for both sides poured in from outside Spain. Those on the Republican side believed it was a contest between democracy and dictatorship, while Nationalist supporters saw it as a battle between order and communist chaos. During the three years the war lasted, around one million Spaniards lost their lives.

Jaume I, who captured Mallorca in 1229

Mallorca and Menorca found themselves on opposite sides. Menorca declared for the Republic and stayed with it to the bitter end. Mallorca's garrison seized the island for the Nationalists. A decisive factor was the presence in Palma of Italian air squadrons, used to bomb Republican Barcelona.

New horizons

Exhausted after the Civil War, Spain remained neutral during World War II and, after the dark years of isolation known as the Noche Negra (Black Night), began a slow economic recovery under Franco's oppressive law-and-order regime, boosted by the growth of the tourism industry.

A small elite had visited the island in the 1920s, but it was in the late 1950s and early 1960s that northern Europeans first began making sun-seeking pilgrimages to Spain, and the Balearic Islands, in any numbers. Tourism transformed the impoverished country's economy, landscape and society. Eager to capitalize, government and private interests poured everything into mass tourism, triggering a rash of uncontrolled and indiscriminate building, with scant regard for tradition or aesthetics. Almost as influential as the financial input was the injection of foreign influences, particularly those associated with the liberalism of the 1960s.

Mallorca, once dependent on agriculture, fishing and small local industries, experienced an explosive growth in tourism and swiftly became one of Europe's most popular holiday destinations.

After the death of General Franco in 1975, his designated successor, the grandson of Alfonso XIII, was crowned King Juan Carlos I. The king managed a smooth transition to democracy, then stood back to allow it full rein. After decades of repression, new freedoms and autonomy were granted to the Spanish regions, and their languages and cultures enjoyed a long-sought renaissance. The Balearic Islands won a degree of autonomy in 1978 and, five years later, became the Comunidad Autónoma de las Islas Baleares. Mallorquín was recognized officially as the language of Mallorca.

Modernization

Spain joined the European Community (now the European Union) in 1986, which gave a further boost to an expanding economy. Mallorca's tourist industry continued to grow, but so did a realization that lack of planning and good taste was leading to damaging long-term consequences – to the environment and to the island's reputation. By the late 1990s, when the 'lager lout' image had become too closely associated with some resorts, production of domestic waste was double the national average, and electricity consumption had increased by 37 percent in five years. It was decided: a new emphasis on quality tourism and safeguarding the environment must take root. Building restrictions were enforced, and a substantial number of areas were declared protected zones.

The economic crisis in 2008 initially sparked a downturn in visitor numbers, but since then, things have picked up considerably, with Mallorca (along with the other Balearic Islands, Ibiza and Menorca) being one of the top tourist destinations in the EU. In 2013, Palma's Pier Ponent was extended to accommodate large cruise ships, and the airport was also enlarged to cope with the increasing number of visitors from outside the EU.

In 2016, the Sustainable Tourism Tax was implemented and subsequently increased in 2019 to fund more sustainable tourism and further protect the island. It's generally reckoned to have been a great success.

Recent years have been marred by the growing opposition to mass tourism, as well as discontent with the high unemployment rate among the younger population. This has sparked regular protests in Palma and across the island, with people calling on the government for greater regulation particularly in the accommodation sector. That said, Mallorca still welcomes tourists with a generous spirit, and responsible visitors should not be put off travelling to the island.

Ferdinand and Isabella greet Christopher Columbus

CREATIVE INPUT

Mallorca has always attracted the creative set. In 1838, Frédéric Chopin and George Sand spent several months in Valldemossa, during which he composed *The Raindrop Prelude* and she wrote *A Winter in Majorca*. Poet and author Robert Graves came to Deià in 1929 and made it his home; he is buried in the little churchyard on the hill. Agatha Christie stayed at *Hotel Illa d'Or* in Port de Pollença in 1932, which inspired her novel *Problems at Pollensa Bay*. Artist Joan Miró, whose wife Pilar was Mallorcan, set up a house and studio in Palma in 1956, rather than live under the Franco regime and he, too, stayed until his death in 1983.

Chronology

c. 1500BC The islanders learn how to work bronze; the Talayotic period begins.

c. 700BC Carthaginians begin to colonize the Balearics.

123BC–400AD Roman occupation; they name the island Balearis Major and establish towns such as Palmaria (Palma) and Pollentia (Alcúdia).

711 Moors land near Gibraltar, and Spain falls under Islamic rule.

848 Moorish rule imposed in the Balearics; it lasts for three hundred years.

1229 Mallorca taken by the Christian army under Jaume I.

1285–87 Alfonso III of Aragón captures Palma.

1349 Jaume III killed in battle by Pere IV of Aragón, ending the Independent Kingdom of Mallorca.

1492 Spain united under the Catholic Monarchs.

1837 First steamship service links Mallorca and Spanish mainland.

1936–39 Spanish Civil War. Mallorca seized by Nationalist forces.

1936–75 Franco's dictatorship; economic hardship in the early years.

1960 Mallorca's airport built. Tourism begins to replace agriculture as the island's main source of income.

1975 Juan Carlos I becomes king after the death of Franco.
1978 Statute of Autonomy gives the Balearic Islands a degree of autonomy; five years later they become an autonomous province and Catalan is restored as the official language.
1986 Spain joins the European Community (now European Union).
1996 The government of the Balearic Islands initiates measures to protect the environment and encourage eco-friendly tourism.
2015 The socialist party (PSIB-PSOE) wins regional elections.
2017 Mallorca passes a law that makes it illegal for bulls to perform for more than ten minutes, or to use sharp implements or have horses in the ring. This makes the sport nearly impossible to stage.
2018 Massive flooding across the eastern part of the island kills at least ten people.
2020–2022 Covid-19 hits Spain hard in the spring; a vaccination programme is rolled out and the epidemic recedes.
2022 Tourism picks up again in Mallorca.
2022 Direct flights between New York and Mallorca are introduced, linking the island with the US in under nine hours.
2025 The Rafa Nadal Museum in Manacor opens a brand-new space dedicated to the Mallorcan tennis champion's success at the French Open.

The Spanish and Balearic flags fly side by side

Sant Elm

Places

Although some visitors to this Mediterranean island arrive by ferry from mainland Spain, the majority land at Palma de Mallorca airport, 12km (7.5 miles) outside the capital. A ring road – the Via Cintura – skirts the city, with roads branching off to the rest of the island; to the craggy, beautiful northwest coast, the quiet, friendly towns peppering the interior plain, the wetlands of S'Albufera in the north, the tiny calas of the east, and the tourist-dominated strips to the east and west of Palma.

Tour agencies offer excursions, by coach or boat, or a combination of the two, to hidden beaches, mountain villages, spectacular caves and weekly markets, but hiring a car (see page 129) is the best way to get around.

The railway options across the island are currently rather limited – the T1 runs to Inca, while the T2 continues to Sa Pobla in the north and the T3 heads to Manacor in the east. A tourist train also trundles along the picturesque railway line from Palma to Sóller. Bus services throughout Mallorca are comprehensive and reliable (see page 139).

Palma de Mallorca

Highlights

- **The Cathedral**, see page 35
- **Palau de l'Almudaina**, see page 37
- **Around the historic centre**, see page 38
- **Patios and museums**, see page 39
- **Moderniste sites**, see page 41
- **Carrer Sant Miquel**, see page 42
- **Passeig d'es Born to the waterfront**, see page 43
- **Out-of-town attractions**, see page 47

Palma's cathedral keeps watch over the harbour

Set around a sheltered bay, **Palma ❶** is a large, cosmopolitan city, with around 486,000 inhabitants – around half the permanent population of Mallorca. It is very much a Mediterranean city, with palm trees and billowing bushes of fragrant oleander, outdoor cafés shaded by colourful awnings, and yachts bobbing alongside working vessels in the bay. Palma is a city with a long history, as the Gothic cathedral towering above the old walls indicates. It's smart and urbane, with designer boutiques, smart restaurants and chic art galleries. Come sundown, the streets spring to life and the city stays awake long into the night.

The old quarter wrapping around the cathedral is perched on a small hill overlooking the bay, and its narrow, atmospheric streets are full of unexpected surprises, from tiny, traditional shops to hidden taverns and hole-in-the-wall bars. To the east of the centre, the Platja de Palma is a long necklace of sandy beaches, sadly scarred by a stretch of concrete from Ca'n Pastilla to S'Arenal. To the west is the seaside promenade of modern Palma, where luxury hotels peer out over a clanking copse of yacht masts, though separated from the harbour by a six-lane highway. Crowning the wooded slopes above the city, where the Spanish royal family have a summer home, are the stone towers of the Castell de Bellver (see page 47).

The Cathedral

Standing proud above the city walls, spectacular when illuminated at night, is the **Cathedral** Ⓐ (www.catedraldemallorca.org; charge). Also known as **La Seu**, this is one of the finest Gothic churches in the whole of Spain. Construction began in 1230 by Jaume I, on the site of the Great Mosque after the Christians recaptured the island from the Moors, but it took nearly four centuries to complete. Densely packed flying buttresses on the south front create an extraordinary effect, especially in the glow of the setting sun, when they are reflected in the lake of the Parc de la Mar below.

WHERE TO SHOOT THE BEST PICTURES

The light in Mallorca is a photographer's friend and the soft evening glow paints exceptional colours over the landscape and stone buildings across the island. Any of the secluded calas are photo worthy but perhaps try Sa Calobra (see page 66) or Cala Llombards on the southeast coast. The towns of Artà (see page 82) and Calvià are well preserved and provide both townscape, historical churches and panoramas. For the iconic Palma cathedral shot, wait until sunset and set up across the lake of Parc de la Mar (see page 44) below the cathedral; try to catch its reflection. As you traverse the island, you'll naturally come across great photo opportunities. Keep an eye out for *miradors* where you'll often capture fine panoramic shots.

The mighty Cathedral, or La Seu

The fourteenth-century **Portal del Mirador** on this same front is a feast of carved stone figurines, including a depiction of *The Last Supper*. Entry is via the Portal de l'Almoina, below the square. Before you step inside, pause to admire the splendid view of the Bay of Palma from the **Mirador** to the south.

The **Museu del Catedral** contains a splendid silver monstrance, some interesting medieval paintings and holy relics. An early Renaissance doorway in carved stone leads into the Baroque Chapter House. The vault of the cathedral's three-aisled, 121m (396ft) interior is supported by slim, elegant pillars. The largest of the seven **rose windows** is magnificent: 12m (40ft) across, composed of 1236 separate sections of stained glass. The extraordinary *baldachin*, a wrought-iron crown of thorns over the high altar, was added by Catalan *Moderniste* architect Antoni Gaudí, creator of Barcelona's Sagrada Família, who worked for ten years on the cathedral in the early twentieth century, though his visits were often short-lived. (*Modernisme* is the Catalan version of Art Nouveau.) The tombs of Jaume II and Jaume III, fourteenth-century kings of Catalunya and Mallorca, are in the Capella de la Trinitat at the east end. The Capella del Santissim is covered with innovative ceramics by Mallorcan artist Miquel Barceló – a six-year labour of love before its much-awaited unveiling in 2007.

To the east of the Cathedral, the **Museu Diocesà** is back in its permanent home in the Bishop's Palace. It contains medieval and Gothic statuary and paintings, along with some lovely stained-glass windows by Gaudí, who lived in the palace while he worked on the Cathedral. The palace itself is well worth a look, too.

Palau de l'Almudaina

The **Palau de l'Almudaina** B (www.patrimonionacional.es; charge) stands just opposite of the cathedral. Once the residence of the Moorish emirs, then of the medieval kings of Mallorca, it is a perfect blend of Islamic and Catalan-Gothic architecture. Highlights include the stone-vaulted throne room, a pretty courtyard (Patio del Rei), a

Palau de l'Almudaina

Gothic chapel (Capella de Santa Anna), and heavily restored royal offices, sometimes used by the present king, where traces of early paintwork survive on the ceilings and walls. There are also some impressive fifteenth- and sixteenth-century Flemish tapestries.

Around the historic centre

In Carrer Palau Reial, to the north of the Almudaina, another palace houses the **Palau March Museu** **C** (www.fundacionbmarch.es; charge). The majestic building and its courtyard houses a small but superb collection of contemporary sculpture, including works by Henry Moore, Barbara Hepworth, Rodin and Chillida, and murals by the Catalan artist Josep Maria Sert, as well as high-quality temporary exhibitions. The palace is also a venue for classical concerts in spring and summer.

The ochre colonnades of the Parliament Building – **Parlament de les Illes Baleares** – run along nearly the full length of Carrer Palau Reial. At the far end, the opulent Renaissance facade of the **Ajuntament** (Town Hall), its overhanging wooden eaves supported by carved beams, dominates **Plaça Cort**. (You can go inside to see the huge processional figures that are stored here). In the centre of the square is an ancient, gnarled olive tree, a favourite spot for photos.

Turn right from the *plaça* and you will reach a pleasant little square, named for the fourteenth-century church of **Santa Eulàlia** **D**, which has a Gothic nave, altar paintings by Francisco Gomez and a clutch of Baroque chapels. Behind the church in the narrow Carrer Can Sanç (off Carrer Carnisseria), the beautifully tiled café of **Can Joan de S'Aigo** (www.

NOTES

In summer, a number of guided tours cover aspects such as *Modernisme*, the Jewish Quarter, the patios, a night tour, and one called Palma Monumental that gives a good historical background. Pick up leaflets from one of the tourist offices.

Basilica de Sant Francesc

canjoandesaigo.com) was artist Joan Miró's favourite place for hot chocolate and almond cake, and is popular with everyone for ice cream.

A right turn brings you to Plaça Quadrado, shaded by palms and plane trees, and with a string of attractive *Moderniste* buildings, the best one being Can Barceló (1902). Above the third-floor oriel windows the facade is decorated with mosaics portraying domestic scenes with women and children. The massive thirteenth-century **Basílica de Sant Francesc** **E** (charge) backs onto Quadrado, and looms above the adjoining Plaça Sant Francesc. A sculpture outside depicts Mallorcan missionary Fray Junípér Serra, founder of the first Californian missions (see page 80). Inside the church, to the left of the Baroque altar, a side-chapel contains the alabaster tomb of Catalan scholar, mystic and missionary Ramón Llull (1235–1316). But the main event is the enchanting Gothic cloister (through which you enter the church), with slender columns, delicate tracery and lemon trees around a central fountain.

Patios and museums

The old quarter of Palma is rich in Renaissance mansions, mostly dating from the sixteenth to the eighteenth centuries, with wonderful patios concealed behind their great wooden doors. Featuring ornate staircases, decorated tiles, palms and potted plants, sometimes cooled by small fountains, they are a delight. Among the best are Can Olesa on Carrer Morey, Can Tacón on Carrer de Sant Jaume II, and Can Bordils (Palma Municipal Archive) and Can Oms, both on Carrer Almudaina.

Most are private or commercial properties, and you have to be content with peeping through the gateways. Alternatively, you can explore a couple of these patios by visiting the museums housed within. On Carrer de la Portella, the renovated Renaissance **Ca La Gran Cristiana** shelters the **Museu de Mallorca** (charge). Exhibits include thirteenth- to sixteenth-century religious paintings, *Moderniste* tiles and twentieth-century paintings. The prehistory and classical archaeology rooms were undergoing long-term refurbishment at the time of writing.

Inside Can Marquès

The former private mansion Can Marqués on Carrer Apuntadors is now the five-star hotel **Palacio Can Marquès**. Originally fifteenth century, the house was mostly furnished and decorated in bourgeois, nineteenth-century style, with some interesting *Moderniste* additions. Following careful renovation, it has been converted into thirteenth unique and luxurious suites, with the interiors designed by New York-based Aline Matsika.

Not far away, on Carrer Can Serra, are the **Banys Àrabs** F (charge), still standing after a thousand years. The courtyard garden is a tranquil, beautiful place when it's not filled with excursion groups. Late afternoon is a good time to visit.

Gran Hotel

Moderniste sites

Alternatively, retrace your steps to Plaça Cort, from where it is only a short walk to the intriguing little shopping streets of Carrer Colom and Jaume II, both of which lead to the deep yellow facades and green shutters of the former marketplace, the **Plaça Major** **G**. The square is busy with cafés, street entertainers and handicraft stalls selling scarves, jewellery and batik work.

Approaching the square, you pass the **Plaça Marquès del Palmer**, where two excellent examples of *Moderniste* architecture – Can Rei and L'Àguila – are adorned with ornate iron grillwork and colourful ceramic flourishes; a café and a smart shoe shop occupy the ground floors.

Down a flight of steps from the Plaça Major, lined with tourist-trap kiosks, Plaça Weyler reveals another pair of fine examples of *Modernisme*. The major one is the imposing **Gran Hotel** **H**, now reimagined as a cultural centre by the **Fundació La Caixa** (www.fundacionlacaixa.org; charge). It includes a bookshop, a smart café-restaurant and an art centre staging excellent exhibitions of contemporary works and permanently housing a display of works by Catalan painter Hermen Anglada Camarasa (1872–1959), who lived in Pollença. This was one of the first modern hotels in Mallorca, built in 1903 by Lluís Doménech i Muntaner. Following a chequered history, La Caixa (Spain's third-largest financial institution) bought it in 1987 and, after renovation works, it reopened in 1993.

Across from the *Gran Hotel* is a small bakery and café, the **Forn des Teatre** (www.fornetdelasoca.com), whose graceful facade graces many a postcard. Down the street, on Plaça Mercat, stand the two gently undulating *Moderniste* buildings that comprise **Can Casasayas**. The bakery took its name from the neighbouring **Teatre Principal**, a grand edifice that stages plays, operas and concerts (see page 103). Follow the road past the theatre and you reach **Via Roma**, an avenue called La Rambla after Barcelona's promenade.

The Forn des Teatre

Carrer Sant Miquel

Turn right from Plaça Major, instead of descending the steps, and you will be in Carrer Sant Miquel, a busy pedestrianized shopping street, home to the **Museu Fundació Joan March** ❶ (www.march.es; free). This striking eighteenth-century building, with marble staircases and stained glass, shelters an exceptional collection belonging to the wealthy March banking family. The seventy-strong permanent display includes works by Picasso, Miró, Dalí, Tàpies and Juan Gris.

THE MARCH DYNASTY

The Fundació March was set up by the extremely wealthy March banking dynasty in 1955 as a philanthropic institution to promote science and culture. You will see branches of the Banca March all over the Balearic Islands, and notice their name appended to numerous cultural ventures. As well as the two major museums mentioned here, there is an extensive library and archive in the Palau March, open to the public as well, and concerts are held there in summer. The foundation funds an annual programme of twentieth-century classical music at Palma's Auditorio and summer concerts in the Jardins March in Cala Ratjada, where there is splendid modern sculpture. Annual prizes for literary criticism and short novels are also awarded by the bank.

Heading north up the street, you will reach the ancient church of **Sant Miquel** – the religious heart of the neighbourhood, a solid building with a fine Baroque altarpiece. A little further on, the deconsecrated church of **Sant Antoniet** opens onto a pretty courtyard that hosts temporary art exhibitions; the walls and pavement outside have become an informal gallery space for local emerging street artists.

Round the corner, on the right, the **Mercat de l'Olivar** ❶ (www.mercatolivar.com) is the city's largest fish, meat and produce market and a popular spot for a tapa or lunch. A very short distance further along Carrer Caputxins is the Plaça d'Espanya, where you will find the Estació Intermodal, the combined rail and bus station.

Passeig d'es Born to the waterfront

If you swerve west instead of north from Plaça Weyler, along traffic-filled Carrer Unió, you come to Plaça Rei Joan Carles I. Ahead is the busy shopping street, Avinguda Jaume III; to your left, the leafy **Passeig des Born**. This broad central avenue, lined with benches and guarded at either end by stone sphinxes, runs down to **Plaça**

Shopping at the market

de la Reina Ⓚ, with a large central fountain. At No. 27, the elegant eighteenth-century **Palau Solleric** (www.casalsolleric.palma.cat; free) houses a cultural foundation and hosts contemporary art exhibitions, plus it also has a café and a tourist information desk.

To the left of Plaça de la Reina (past the tourist office), steps lead up to the cathedral, where our tour began. Hugging the old city walls, **S'Hort del Rei** is a lovely Arabic-style garden dotted with fountains and pools, which makes a pleasant distraction from city traffic. Miró's beloved **Personatge** sculpture, *The Egg*, stands on the corner nearest the *plaça*. Facing it is the cool and minimalist café that is part of the Palau March. Parallel to S'Hort del Rei, a much-needed car park was built beneath a stretch of the Avinguda Antoni Maura. Below the city walls, on the southern side, the attractively landscaped **Parc de la Mar** forms a barrier against the coastal motorway, the **Passeig Marítim**. The park has an artificial lake and modern sculptures, including works by Miró, and is the venue for free open-air concerts on summer evenings, as is Ses Voltes, lying directly beneath the cathedral walls.

A right turn here leads to the turreted **Sa Llotja** Ⓛ (open only if there are exhibitions; free) in the square of the same name. Designed in the fifteenth century by Guillem Sagrera (after whom this stretch of the Passeig Marítim is named), it was once the merchants' stock exchange, and is one of Spain's finest civic Gothic buildings, with slim columns twisting through a light-flooded interior to the vaulted roof. It is now used for art exhibitions. Nearby, **Plaça Drassana** is a pleasant if somewhat shabby neighbourhood square. Back on the main coastal road, the seventeenth-century **Consolat de Mar**, the former maritime law court, is the HQ of the president of the Balearic Islands' government. The two buildings are linked by the Porta del Mar, one of the old city gates. The maze of narrow streets between Plaça de Sa Llotja and Plaça de la Reina forms Palma's lively restaurant and nightlife area.

Cross the road at the nearest traffic lights to explore Palma's harbour and waterfront. You'll probably spot fishermen mending their nets (although the fishing fleet is not what it was), smart yachts around the **Real Club Náutic** (www.rcnp.es), opportunities to take boat trips around the harbour, and, at the western end, the car ferry passenger terminal. En route, several pleasant cafés and restaurants gaze out over the port, while cyclists, runners and rollerbladers whizz past on a designated track. The harbourfront is planted with palms, hibiscus and oleander, but there is no ignoring the fact that six lanes of traffic are roaring past on the other side. Nonetheless, it is very pleasant on a summer

Miró's Personatge sculpture

evening, when the sun sets over the water and the illuminated cathedral glows before you.

Back from the waterfront, almost opposite the Real Club Náutic, the prestigious **Es Baluard Museu d'Art Modern i Contemporani** Ⓜ (www.esbaluard.org; charge) is housed in a stunning white structure built into the city fortifications in Plaça Porta de Santa Catalina. Its temporary exhibitions change regularly, while its permanent collection includes works by Picasso, Miró and Tàpies as well as Mallorcan artists Miquel Barceló and Juli Ramis on display. The views of the port and the city from the rooftop and terrace are impressive. Classical music recitals are held in the museum on some evenings.

Castell de Bellver

Out-of-town attractions

Moorish-style arches at the Poble Espanyol

Further west, there are three more places worth mentioning. The **Poble Espanyol** (N) (www.puebloespanolmallorca.com; charge), a walled town of replica architectural treasures from across Spain, is kitsch but entertaining. The buildings house shops, craft studios, bars and cafés. It is reached on foot (twenty minutes from the city centre) or by buses #5, #29, #46 (Andrea Doria bus stop) and #50 (Bus Turistic).

Just south of the Poble Espanyol, perched on a hilltop, is the **Castell de Bellver** (O) (www.castelldebellver.palma.es; charge), reached on bus #50 (Bus Turistic). A magnificent example of Gothic military architecture, the stronghold has commanded the approaches to the city since the fourteenth century. From the battlements, the view of the city and the bay is stunning. Inside, the small **Museu d'Història de la Ciutat** traces the history and archaeology of the area.

The best of the bunch, though, is the **Fundació Pilar i Joan Miró** (P) (www.miromallorca.com; charge but free on Saturdays after 3pm and the first Sunday of each month) on Carrer Joan de Saridakis in the suburb of Cala Major. Bus #4 or #46 will take you right to the door, but a taxi from the centre is not too expensive. The Catalan artist and his Mallorcan wife lived on the island, from

1956 until his death in 1983, and the foundation displays a fine selection of his work.

The western corner

Highlights

- **West of the bay**, see page 49
- **Port d'Andratx and Sant Elm**, see page 50
- **Up the scenic coast**, see page 51
- **La Granja**, see page 52

When tourism hit Mallorca, the Bay of Palma, with two magnificent sweeps of white sand almost 30km (18 miles) long, was irresistible, and the resorts that mushroomed along here in the 1960s and 1970s gave the island a name for cheap and cheerful holidays. The picture soon turned decidedly tacky, dominated by package tourism and high-rise hotels, though in recent years, the Balearic government has done its best to move everything upmarket.

Portals Vells

To the west of the bay, there's less intense development after Camp de Mar, where the coast road winds through forest to Port d'Andratx. After a detour to Sant Elm, at the island's southwestern tip, there is a beautiful winding coastal road to the village of Banyalbufar. Then head inland via the La Granja estate and La Reserva Puig de Galatzó, after which you can complete the loop back to Palma or continue up the picturesque west coast.

NOTES

The region of Calvià – home to the ever-popular resorts of Magaluf, Palma Nova and Santa Ponça – has really made strides in tidying up the image of Mallorca and is pushing sustainable practices. The council has converted all beach showers to filtered seawater to cut down on usable water waste.

West of the bay

You can either take the Via Cintura (ring road Ma-20), which becomes the Ma-1 motorway at Porto Pi, or the coast road. Either way, you will see a turn-off to **Cala Major** (where the Spanish royal family has their summer home). The coastal road wends through the resorts of **Sant Agustí**, with its small yacht harbour, and crowded **Ses Illetes**, to a rocky stretch of coast and the exclusive **Bendinat** and **Portals Nous**. Here, apartments cluster on the slopes and a glamorous marina, **Puerto Portals**, has been carved out of the cliffs.

Sandy beaches start again at the resorts of **Costa d'en Blanes** – home to the popular aquarium, **Marineland** – and **Palma Nova**, which blends almost imperceptibly into **Magaluf**. The wide, sandy beach here abounds with a solid block of bronzing bodies by day, and the town centre is lively by night. Over the past few years, huge investment has been poured into Magaluf to shake off its gaudy reputation, and while there are still hangovers – in more ways than one – from the hedonistic days of the 1990s and early 2000s, the resort is now much more suited to families and couples. The waterfront promenade has undergone major refurbishment and is lined with exclusive beach clubs such as *Nikki Beach* (www.nikkibeach.com/mallorca).

Port d'Andratx

A pine-flanked road runs south to the pretty cove of **Portals Vells** ❷, which has somehow escaped overdevelopment. The cliffs are honeycombed with caverns dating from prehistoric times, enlarged over the centuries. Boats make the short excursion from the pier at Magaluf, so it's not always peaceful. Its neighbour, El Mago, was Mallorca's first nudist beach. Not far south of Portals Vells, you can walk to the tranquil cove of **Cala Figuera** – one of three on the island with the same name – but the end of the peninsula is an abandoned military base that is almost entirely cloaked in graffiti. Discussions are ongoing about whether to demolish it.

Port d'Andratx and Sant Elm

Back at Magaluf, pick up the motorway and turn off at Camp de Mar, where a scenic road twists through pine forest to **Port**

d'Andratx ❸. More yachts than fishing boats bob on the calm waters of the bay these days. The old harbour area still looks traditional, but a string of chic restaurants and shops lines the waterfront, and villas and apartments climb the slopes across the water. The lack of a sandy beach has kept the big hotels and package tours away, however, and the vibe remains relaxed.

The quiet inland town of Andratx plays host to the impressive **CCA Andratx Art Contemporani** (www.ccandratx.eu; charge), the brainchild of a cool Danish couple, which stages contemporary art exhibitions and runs artists' workshops. This is the largest contemporary art centre in Mallorca. From here, you could divert to **Sant Elm ❹**, the island's westernmost point, a former fishing village that has clung on to its identity, though sailors, surfers and divers have known about it for a long time. Offshore, the nature-reserve island of **Sa Dragonera** (www.sadragonera.org) can be visited almost every day by boat. Check the boat company's website for departure details (www.crucerosmargarita.com; charge).

Up the scenic coast

From Andratx, the Ma-10 wiggles across the southern reaches of the **Serra de Tramuntana**, around numerous hairpin bends to the coast, where it wends between the ocean and the clifftops. To the right, terraces are planted with fruit trees and olives, surrounding a string of delightful little villages. Along the road are a succession of *miradors*, viewpoints framing commanding coastal vistas; one or two still crowned with ancient watchtowers from which lookouts once scanned the sea for pirate ships. The **Mirador Es Grau ❺** has fantastic views of the coast, and a huge restaurant in which to sit and enjoy them.

Estellencs, some 4km (2.5 miles) on, is an ancient village set among orange groves on the slopes of Puig de Galatzó (1027m/3370ft). From the town, you can walk or drive down a track to a little fishing cove. Another 5km (3 miles) further on, the sixteenth-century **Torre del Verger** offers one of the finest views of the coast. The next town, **Banyalbufar** ❻ is a pretty place with Moorish origins. The Arabic name means 'vineyard by the sea', and it is still famous for its terraced hillsides – and a popular haunt for artists. There are a couple of pleasant hotels, a cluster of restaurants, and a lane that twists down to a rocky cove whose crystal-clear water is ideal for diving.

La Granja

North of Banyalbufar, the road swerves inland, in the direction of **Esporles**, and from here, you can return to Palma on the Ma-1120, continue up the west coast, or take the minor road to Puigpunyent

The manor house at La Granja

to visit **La Reserva Puig de Galatzó** ❼ (www.reservapark.net; charge). A tangle of 3km (2 miles) of paths wraps around waterfalls and caves, weaving through protected land rich in bird and animal life, on the lush slopes of Galatzó, known as the mystical mountain because of its magnetic properties. The trails are fairly easy, though you will need sensible shoes. For something more adventurous you can try abseiling, climbing, mountain biking, ziplining and crossing rope bridges.

The west coast

Highlights

This is one of the most dramatic and beautiful routes in Mallorca. It's hard to pick a highlight as there are so many, from Valldemossa, where George Sand and Frédéric Chopin once stayed, to the lovely hilltop village of Deià; the former home of poet Robert Graves; the clifftop mansion of the Habsburg Archduke Ludwig; and the agreeable town of Sóller.

Whether you are continuing a route round the coast on the Ma-10 or coming direct from Palma on the Ma-1110 – a good, relatively straight road, running through groves of olives and almonds – your first stop will be Valldemossa. As you approach, the incline becomes steeper until the village and monastery suddenly appear, like something out of a fairytale.

La Real Cartuja de Valldemossa

Although **Valldemossa** ❽ was the birthplace of Mallorca's only home-grown saint, Catalina Tomás, it was the visit of French writer George Sand – Amandine-Aurore-Lucile Dupin – and her lover, Frédéric Chopin, in the winter of 1838 to 1839 that really put the town on the map. They don't seem to have been very happy here, however; Chopin was unwell, the weather was miserable, and the villagers disapproved of Sand's habit of wearing men's clothes and smoking cigars. In return, she disparaged the local people in her book, *A Winter in Majorca*, calling them 'barbarians and thieves', although she thought that Mallorca was 'the most beautiful place I have ever lived'.

Valldemossa monastery

Nowadays, coachloads of visitors disturb the peace of this little hilltop town as they flock to see the couple's lodgings in the former Carthusian monastery, **La Real Cartuja de Valldemossa** (www.cartoixadevalldemossa.com; charge). The monastery was founded in 1399, but when the monks were expelled in 1835, some of their cells were sold as apartments – although the 'cells' were in fact three-room suites with private gardens. Those rented by Sand and Chopin are now a museum, displaying manuscripts, Chopin's death mask and his piano. You can also visit the massive church, the pharmacy, with a beautiful collection of eighteenth-century ceramic jars, the library and the Prior's Cell. There is an interesting **Museu Municipal** here, too, with documents relating to the Archduke Ludwig; and an **art gallery** displaying paintings by Joan Miró, Max Ernst and Antoni Saura as well as Mallorcan landscapes.

Chopin's death mask, among memorabilia at the monastery

The adjoining sixteenth-century palace, the **Palau Sancho** was constructed on the site of one Jaume II built for his son, Sancho, and is entered via a tranquil, plant-filled courtyard. Piano recitals of Chopin's music are held throughout the day, and Festival Chopin takes place here every August.

Around the town

Outside the monastery is a cobbled *plaça* shaded with lime trees – *tilos* – which give the square its name. The streets around it, and those leading to the thirteenth-century church of Sant Bartomeu, dedicated to Santa Catalina, are bright with potted plants, and the steepest, most slippery parts are covered with strips of carpet to prevent people tripping up.

The main street in the lower town, where there are adequate car parks, is lined with cafés, restaurants and interesting little shops selling jewellery and clothes made of cool, natural fibres. One of the nicest bars (just back from the main street, on Carrer Blanquera) serves delicious *horchata* (milky drink made from rice or tiger nuts), fresh juice and good coffee and hot chocolate, along with *cocas de patata*, the sugar-dusted, potato-shaped buns, tasting not unlike *ensaïmadas*, which are a local speciality.

In the other direction, a few metres along the road towards Banyalbufar, a vertiginous road plummets 6km (4 miles) to the tiny **Port de Valldemossa**, where there's a small gravel beach and crystal-clear water. On summer weekends, however, the narrow road and the limited parking area become uncomfortably busy.

Son Marroig

The coastal Ma-10 presses north, with stunning sea views to the left, and groves of ancient, gnarled olive trees among huge boulders to the right. After about 6km (4 miles), a track signposted simply **Miramar** leads to the ruins of a monastery founded by Ramon Lull. Only part of the cloister remains, but there's also a chapel and

CATALINA TOMÁS

Santa Catalina is Mallorca's very own saint. She was born in Valldemossa in 1531 in a house at Carrer Rectoría 5, behind the church, and this is now a tiny shrine. In a quiet corner of Carrer de la Beatà, where caged birds sing, there is another smaller shrine with a fountain and ferns. Almost every house has a tiled picture outside, depicting scenes from the saint's life and asking her blessing: 'Santa Catalina Tomás Pregau Per Nosaltres'. She was a farmer's daughter, marked out as special when still a child, and taken to Palma by a sympathetic patron, where she worked as a servant in a wealthy household before entering the convent of Santa Magdalena and taking her vows.

Archduke Ludwig's former mansion, Son Marroig

a museum with artefacts collected by Archduke Ludwig. A short way further on, a sign points to **Son Marroig** ❾ (www.sonmarroig.com; charge), a manor house that belonged to the Austrian Archduke Ludwig Salvator of Habsburg-Lorraine and Bourbon, who had a life-long love affair with the Balearics and their people. Born in Florence in 1847, he renounced courtly life in Vienna and spent years travelling the world on scientific explorations, returning often to the estate he bought in 1870 on this beautiful stretch of coast. Several rooms, filled with paintings, photos and ceramics, can be visited. In the gardens, there's a wonderful view from a cliff-edge white temple made of Carrara marble.

Hundreds of metres below the house, **Sa Foradada** is a rocky promontory pierced by a remarkable 18m (60ft)-wide natural window. If you visit the house, ask for permission to make the

Honey-hued town of Deià

half-hour walk down to the sea and the landing stage where the archduke used to anchor his yacht, the *Nixe*. The restaurant near the car park is a wonderful place from which to watch the sunset. Concerts are held at Son Marroig during the Deià International Music Festival (www.dimf.com; see page 106).

Deià

Set on the slopes of the 1064m (3491ft) Teix massif, **Deià** ⑩ is a pretty town of honey-coloured stone that's lured artists, writers and assorted expatriates ever since the Archduke Ludwig first came here. He was followed by the Catalan poet and painter Santiago Rusinyol at the turn of the twentieth century, and later by writer Anaïs Nin (1903–77) and the American archaeologist William Waldren. But it is Robert Graves (1895–1985), the poet and author of *I, Claudius* and the autobiographical *Goodbye to All That*, who came here with American writer Laura Riding in 1929, that is most closely associated with the place. Graves loved Deià and fiercely defended the northwest coast against commercial exploitation. His home, **Ca N'Alluny** (www.lacasaderobertgraves.org; charge) on the Carretera Deià–Sóller has been restored and opened as a museum. The house and garden are delightful and retain much of their original character as well as exhibiting the writer's effects.

You must leave your car on the main street, which is lined with restaurants, galleries and shops. Narrow, winding streets lead to the top of the village and the little church of **Sant Joan Baptista**. Beside it, a small cemetery overlooks the Mediterranean; a simple cement slab bears the inscription 'Robert Graves, Poeta, E.P.D.'.

Deià is extremely popular, and a well-heeled crowd have set up holiday homes here. Besides a luxury hotel, *La Residencia A Belmond Hotel* (www.belmond.com), there is a handful of wallet-friendly alternatives and the best selection of restaurants on the coast (see page 121).

Port de Sóller

Cala Deià

Just past the village, a twisting 2km (1 mile) drive takes you down to **Cala Deià**, a tiny cove with a rocky beach, where ramps emerge

NOTES

Sóller is a good place to try freshly squeezed orange juice (*zumo de naranja*), as the citrus groves around the town are reputed to produce the best in the Mediterranean. You could also sample the local orange liqueur, called *àngel d'or*, which is used to flavour some of the cakes found on menus and in Sóller's many tempting bakeries.

from boathouses set into the cliffs. The water is clear, buoyant and safe, and there are a couple of reasonable beach cafés. Don't imagine you've found a secluded beach, though. Regular visitors know it well, and it can get very busy at weekends. You can walk to the beach, either by following steps near the vehicle-access road, or via the steep Carrer Bauza at the Valldemossa end of the village, tracing the course of a stream past pretty gardens until the houses peter out and the path continues through groves of lemons and olives; it takes about 35 minutes in all.

Sóller and its port

From Deià, the coast road, lined with citrus and almond groves and vineyards, descends into the broad valley of Sóller. The scenery is lovely, and the town of **Sóller** ⓫ itself is a little gem, a busy, prosperous place that claims, like several others, to have been the birthplace of Columbus. It is full of well-preserved eighteenth- and nineteenth-century mansions, and the main, café-lined square, **Plaça Sa Constitució**, is a good place to sit and absorb the town's character. Like the old main street, the Gran Via, the square has *Moderniste* (Catalan Art Nouveau) flourishes, including the church of **Sant Bartomeu**, and the former Banco Central Hispano (now Banco Santander) on the opposite corner, whose exteriors were designed by a pupil of Antoni Gaudí. About five minutes' walk to the east is **Can Prunera** (http://canprunera.com; charge), a fine old mansion turned museum dedicated to the *Moderniste* movement.

The train station at the top of the town is another splendid *Moderniste* building. You can make an old-fashioned journey on a little wooden train – Ferrocarril de Sóller (www.trendesoller.com; charge) – that's been trundling to Palma on a narrow-gauge railway since 1912.

The station has another attraction: the **Sala Miró y Sala Picasso** (free), hung with drawings and lithographs by Miró and filled with a display of some fifty ceramic pieces by Picasso.

Outside the station, you can pick up information on hiking (*senderisme*) from the tourist office, housed in an old train carriage. Here, too, you can catch the vintage **tram** that rattles on a scenic, twenty-minute journey to **Port de Sóller** (www.trendesoller.

Cala de Deià

Sóller's vintage tram

com; charge), stopping en route where requested. The port is a good old-fashioned resort with a fine harbour, and it has gained a crop of smart restaurants and bars in recent years. You can hire kayaks, sign up for sailing or windsurfing lessons, and take boat trips around the bay or further afield to Sa Calobra and Sa Foradada.

Two gardens

Just outside town, beside the ring road, the **Museu Balear de Ciències Naturales i Jardí Botànic** (mucbo.org; charge) shelters a collection of aromatic herbs and plants from all over the Balearic Islands, fossils, a vegetable garden and a 'peace garden'.

The road from Sóller to Palma, with numerous hairpin bends negotiating the 496m (1627ft) **Coll de Sóller**, was believed to be impeding the local economy and consequently, in the 1990s, a tunnel was drilled through the mountains. This slashed travel time to Palma to around half an hour; a private company built the tunnel and made a fortune from a toll, though this was removed in 2017.

At the southern exit from the tunnel (on the left), the **Jardins d'Alfàbia** ⓬ (www.jardinesdealfabia.com; charge) are the wonderful gardens of a baronial mansion that was once the country estate of a Moorish vizier of Pollença. The cisterns, fountains and irrigation channels are a bit neglected, but the flowing water and shaded walks, with turkeys pecking beneath fig trees and birds singing among exotic plants, are appealing. The house is packed with treasures: look out for the huge fourteenth-century oak chair regarded as one of the most important antiques in Mallorca.

From Bunyola to Castell d'Alaró

A few kilometres past the gardens, a left-hand turn points to **Bunyola**, a peaceful little place that produces excellent olive oil and a bright green herbal liqueur called Palo Tunel. The village church and the town hall both stand on the main square, Sa Plaça, shaded by leafy plane trees. It's a lovely drive from here to the tiny village of **Orient**, which has a hotel (plus a few in the nearby area) and several restaurants and is a favourite base for hikers. The

Mountain village in the Serra de Tramuntana

Castell d'Alaró

Castell d'Alaró ⓭, a ruined fortress built by Jaume I, crowns a massive crag 822m (2700ft) high.

You can walk up from Orient if you have bags of energy, strong shoes and plenty of drinking water, or drive most of the way to the summit up narrow, tortuous lanes, starting a little north of the nearby town of **Alaró**. The tracks become progressively rougher, however, and the final stretch is only suitable for 4WDs. Park before this section begins, at the restaurant *Es Verger*, and look for a sign saying 'Castell a Peu' (To the castle on foot). That leaves a forty-minute climb to reach the summit, not advisable in the heat of summer. The views from the top are spectacular. There is a small restaurant and simple accommodation, which must be booked in advance (www.caminsdepedra.conselldemallorca.es).

The heart of the Tramuntana

If you head in the opposite direction from Sóller, towards Pollença, the magnificent views continue as the road cuts through the heart of the UNESCO-listed Serra de Tramuntana, with **Puig Major** – Mallorca's highest mountain at 1445m (4741ft) – rising high above.

Fornalutx ⓮ is an exquisite little town of warm stone buildings that's been designated a national monument – which naturally means it draws a lot of visitors, but also means building regulations are stringent. Set against the backdrop of the Tramuntana range, its steep, cobbled streets are lined with cacti and palm trees. A high proportion of the well-restored medieval properties belong to overseas investors, attracted by the region's beauty. The town is set among ancient terraces of citrus fruits and silver-leaved olive trees, marked out with dry-stone walls. Paths run through them to pretty little **Biniaraix**, which is also only a half-hour walk down narrow lanes, signposted from the centre of Sóller.

A short distance past Fornalutx on the Ma-10, the **Mirador de Ses Barques** has a restaurant where you can stop for a drink or bite to eat while enjoying spectacular views of Port de Sóller and the coast. The route then winds past the reservoirs of Panta de

Fornalutx

Cycling near Sa Calobra

Cúber and Panta de GorgBlau, connected by a narrow canal. Near the latter, a little road leads down to the coast at **Sa Calobra** ⓯. This is one of the most dramatic drives on the island, a serpentine 12km (8 mile) -long route of near-continuous hairpin bends that zigzag down to sea level. The views are stunning, and the road is an adventure in itself, but try to come early in the morning to avoid the streams of tourist coaches.

Park where you can when the road reaches sea level and walk a short distance towards the deep gorge of **Torrent de Pareis**. Tunnels burrow through the rock to the riverbed, where the chasm widens into a huge natural amphitheatre. Be extra careful if it has rained, even only a little, as the rocks get very slippery. The idyllic little bay, **Cala de Sa Calobra**, has a couple of restaurants and bars and a pebbly beach, but they get very crowded in summer.

Monestir de Lluc

Around 10km (6 miles) further along the road to Pollença is the major pilgrimage site in Mallorca, the **Santuari de Lluc** ⓰ (www.lluc.net). Located in a valley near Puig des Castellot, the massive abode mainly dates from the eighteenth century, but pilgrims have been coming here since the thirteenth century to pray to a dark-stone statue of the Madonna and Child, La Moreneta. According to legend, it was discovered by an Arab boy called Lluc, whose family had converted to Christianity. He took the statue to the church of Sant Pere in the tiny village of Escorça nearby, but it kept returning to the place where he had found it, so it was finally allowed to stay, and a chapel was built to house it.

People still come to venerate La Moreneta, but many also come to have lunch and admire the views, as the monastery has a restaurant, bar and barbecue area. It also offers inexpensive accommodation; the rooms are pretty basic, but staying here allows you to appreciate the peace of the monastery once the tour groups have gone home. If you attend Mass in the church during the school year, you will have the pleasure of hearing the Lluc boys' and girls' choir, **Els Blavets** (Blue Ones), named after the colour of their cassocks. They also sing in the evenings, on Sundays and at special services.

Heading north

Highlights

- **Pollença,** see page 68
- **Cala Sant Vicenç and Port de Pollença,** see page 72
- **Cap de Formentor** , see page 73
- **Alcúdia,** see page 75
- **Port d'Alcúdia and the bay,** see page 76
- **Parc Natural de S'Albufera,** see page 77

The cockerel on the fountain is a symbol of Pollença

The north is a region of great diversity. It encompasses the rugged Cap de Formentor, the sandy coves of Sant Vicenç, two attractive towns – Pollença and Alcúdia – the resort of Port de Pollença and the huge, curved Badia d'Alcúdia, lined with resorts and facilities. Parallel to the bay is a complete contrast in the wetlands of the Parc Natural de S'Albufera.

From Palma, it is a fast drive up the Ma-13 motorway to the Ma-2200 turning to Pollença. If continuing the previous route, the road from Lluc curves through tranquil holm oak forests before descending to the Vall de Son Marc and Pollença.

Pollença

Pollença ⓱ has a long history. The Romans may have established a small settlement here (see page 75), and the stone bridge to the north of the town centre is believed to have been built by them, though the actual origin of the edifice is still up for some debate. The Catalan community was founded in 1236 after the Moors were expelled. Present-day Pollença was first shown on a map in 1789; it was a prosperous town, for a while the feudal property of the Knights Templar, and able to support the numerous impressive churches still standing.

Pollença is a lively place, especially during summer evenings, when it teems with visitors; the comings and goings in the **Plaça Major** provide free entertainment for people sipping cool drinks outside one of several cafés and restaurants. The *plaça* also comes into its own on Sunday morning, when local people shop for fresh produce in the market, then drink coffee outside *Café Espanyol* (also called *Ca'n Moixet*), after attending Mass in the parochial church, **La Mare de Déu des Àngels**.

The Carrer de Monte-Sion, leading off the square towards the Jesuit church of the same name, has some great little shops and a clutch of restaurants. Ceramics can be found in *Ceràmiques Monti-Sion*, which offers an excellent range of handcrafted pieces in both

Santuari de Lluc

PUIG DE SANTA MARIA

Just outside Pollença on the Palma road, a path leads up to the **Santuari del Puig**, the medieval convent on top of the 330m (1083ft) -high **Puig de Santa Maria**. The first half of the 4km (2-mile) trail can be tackled by car if you have nerves of steel; the latter part only on foot. The dry-stone walls (*margers*) along the last section are a good demonstration of an ancient skill that is now dying out. The views from the top, stretching as far as the Serra de Tramuntana, Cap de Formentor, the plain of Sa Pobla and the bays of Alcúdia and Pollença, are superb. The fourteenth-century Gothic convent began as a plea for protection against the Black Death but quickly became one of the most sacred buildings on the island. Accommodation is available and there is a bar and a restaurant.

traditional and modern designs. Nearby is little Plaça de l'Almoina; the fountain has a cockerel on top, the symbol of the town. In Carrer Roca, the **Fundació i Casa Museu Dionís Bennassar** (www.fdionis.org; charge) displays the work and personal possessions of this local artist (1904–67) in his family home.

From the parish church in the *plaça* (or from the Ajuntament, off to the left), the **Via Crucis** (Way of the Cross), a flight of 365 steps lined with cypress trees, leads to **El Calvari**. This little chapel has been given a rhyming name – **La Mare de Déu del Peu de la Creu** (Mother of God at the Foot of the Cross) – after a fourteenth-century sculpture inside showing Mary at the feet of Christ. At the foot of the steps, the **Museu Martí Vicenç** (www.martivicens.org) exhibits the works of the local artist, sculptor and textile designer.

Back in town, the deconsecrated Dominican convent and church of **Sant Domingo** is now a temple to culture rather than worship. Exhibitions of installation art are staged in the nave of the great seventeenth-century church in summer, and the cloisters are the venue for a classical music festival in July or August (see page

106), when an international line-up of orchestras and soloists performs. Pollença's **Museu Municipal** (free) is also housed inside the monastery in a large, light space. Somewhat eclectic, it includes changing exhibitions of contemporary paintings and sculpture, a permanent collection of Gothic art, some early twentieth-century paintings and a smattering of archaeological finds.

Outside the convent, the **Jardins Joan March Severa**, built around a watchtower and an antique water wheel, has an interesting collection of Balearic plants. The garden is always open, but the watchtower is not accessible. Carrer Roser Vell leads off to the left; at its far end you will see the plain facade of the little fourteenth-century oratory of **Roser Vell**.

Port de Pollença

Cala Sant Vicenç

Cala Sant Vicenç and Port de Pollença

About 3km (2 miles) along the Ma-2200 from Pollença to its port is the turning to **Cala Sant Vicenç** ⑱, a family resort built around three sandy coves with brilliant blue water, excellent for swimming and snorkelling – although strong winds can pick up quite quickly.

A couple more kilometres along the main road brings you to **Port de Pollença**. Tucked into the wide curve of a bay, with the marina in the centre, it has been popular with English visitors for many years and retains a distinctive atmosphere. However, it is a resort with an alter-ego. To the north of the marina, the promenade has a plethora of restaurants, some with tables spilling onto the sands, and a couple of stylish hotels. These give way to old, one-storey houses and wooden jetties, where the branches of trees almost reach the water. To the south of the marina, however, the palm-shaded promenade that flanks the lovely, long sweep of sandy beach is lined wall-to-wall with cheap and cheerful tripper shops and fast-food joints. The narrow streets unfurling from behind the northerly promenade are nicer. There's a lot to do, though: sailing and scuba lessons are on offer, and there are boat trips to Formentor and Cala Sant Vicenç.

Cap de Formentor

Continuing round the bay to the southeast, towards Alcúdia, the commercial zone ends abruptly, and the beach narrows to a sliver, popular with windsurfers, with an expanse of lonely wetlands unfurling the other side.

But before heading in this direction, make a diversion to the island's northernmost point, **Cap de Formentor** ⓳, the slender headland on the north side of the Badia de Pollença. With sheer cliffs and an idyllic sandy beach, the rocky peninsula, caressed by clear turquoise waters, is simply spectacular. The best place to appreciate the extraordinary landscape is the **Mirador de la Creueta**, about 5km (3 miles) from Port de Pollença, where there is a specially designed walkway to make the most of this vantage point. Some tour buses don't trudge any further than this, which is a blessing for motorists, as the twisting road is a challenging one, demanding much concentration, and can get swamped with traffic in summer.

Just beyond the Mirador de la Creueta, the pretty, pine-shaded beach

NOTES

On the promenade north of the marina, you may notice a memorial bust of Hermen Anglada Camarasa (1872–1959), the Catalan *Moderniste* painter after whom this stretch is named. He lived and worked in Pollença for many years. A collection of his work can be seen in the CaixaForum in the old *Gran Hotel* in Palma (see page 41).

(signposted Platja de Formentor on the right-hand side) is a favourite picnic spot and offers splendid views across the bay – similar to those from the exclusive *Hotel Formentor*, owned by the luxury hospitality giant *Four Seasons* (www.fourseasons.com/mallorca). The hotel was built in 1928 by an Argentinian architect, Adam Diehl, and quickly became popular with a fashionable set, which included the Duke of Windsor and Mrs Simpson, Sir Winston Churchill and the Rainiers of Monaco.

From the beach turn-off, it's another 12km (8 miles) to the lighthouse at the tip. Just before you enter the tunnel that leads through El Fumat, there's a great view of the sparkling waters of the Badia de Pollença glistening far below.

Cap de Formentor

Alcúdia

Retrace your steps past Port de Pollença to the ancient, walled town of **Alcúdia** ⓴. There were Phoenician and Greek settlements here before the Romans founded their city in 123BC and called it Pollentia. The Vandals sacked it, the Moors rebuilt it – Al Kudia (means 'on the hill') – and the conquering Spaniards fortified it in the thirteenth century. The sturdy walls and gates before you are later imitations, but still impressive. Today, it's an inviting, unpretentious little place, with some excellent Renaissance facades; good cafés and restaurants on the central **Plaça Constitució**; and a lively market on Tuesdays and Sundays, held just outside the city walls.

Neo-Gothic church of Sant Jaume

The sturdy neo-Gothic church of **Sant Jaume**, which has a lovely rose window and Baroque altars, forms the southern bastion in the walls. Opposite the church, a small, fourteenth-century building shelters the **Museo Monogràfic de Pollentia** (charge). It has an extensive collection of Roman finds, including ceramics, glassware, tools and surgical instruments. You can pick up a free leaflet here, describing points of interest in the Roman city. The remains of that city, the **Ciutat Romana del Pollentia**, excavated in the 1950s by members of a dig organized by American archaeologist William Bryant, stand outside the walls (there's a large car park and a bus from Palma stops nearby). The area includes remnants of several

Alfresco dining in Alcúdia

buildings and gives a good idea of the town's layout. The star turn, however, is the substantial remains of the **Teatre Romà** (Roman Theatre), dating from the first century BC.

Port d'Alcúdia and the bay

Port d'Alcúdia has evolved from a small fishing harbour into an all-purpose port for commercial, naval and pleasure craft, and is one of the largest resorts on the north coast. Restaurants, cafés and clubs have mushroomed rapidly, as have high-rise hotels and apartment blocks, which now spread around the bay to form an almost unbroken ribbon of buildings 10km (6 miles) long.

To the east of the port, on a wide and rocky headland, is the Museu Sa Bassa Blanca, formerly the Fundació Yannick y Ben Jakober (www.msbb.org; charge), which displays portraits of children from the sixteenth to the nineteenth centuries. There is also a collection of contemporary art and a sculpture park.

In summer, the stretch of glorious white-sand beaches abutting **Port d'Alcúdia** is a mass of bodies soaking up the sun's rays or sheltering beneath colourful umbrellas. Although big, crowded and impersonal, the resort, which more or less merges into Ca'n Picafort at the eastern end, does not have the seediness of some of the southern spots. Both remain low-key, if perhaps a bit soulless, and are good options for families with children or teenagers in need of entertainment. The water here is clear and safe and incredibly shallow, so ideal for younger kids.

As you drive along the main road, flanked by supermarkets, shops and high-rise hotels, signs saying simply '*platja*' lead to the beach. The area around **Platja de Muro** is a bit quieter, but not by much.

Parc Natural de S'Albufera

Parc Natural de S'Albufera

About halfway between Port d'Alcúdia and Can Picafort, almost opposite the *Hotel Parc Natural* (www.grupotel.com), is the entrance to the **Parc Natural de S'Albufera** ㉑ (free). There's a car park a few metres further from the entrance. It seems remarkable to find this huge swathe of wetlands so close to major resorts, and it can be a real haven

Just one of Mallorca's 'thousand windmills'

for visitors as well as for birds, more than two hundred species of which have been spotted here. A free permit must be picked up from the Reception Centre, about 1km (0.5 miles) from the entrance. The reserve sprawls across 800 hectares (2000 acres), threaded by walking and cycling tracks and crisscrossed by a network of canals constructed in the nineteenth century by a British company that began reclaiming marshland for agriculture, but ran out of money. The area became a protected zone in 1988, one of the first beneficiaries of the new environmental consciousness.

The Plain

Highlights

- **Sa Pobla**, see page 79
- **Binissalem and Sineu**, see page 79
- **From Petra to the sanctuaries**, see page 80

Bounded by mountains and hills to the north and east, the central portion of Mallorca is called **Es Pla** (The Plain). Lightly populated and not particularly geared towards visitors, there are lovely agricultural landscapes studded with ancient stone farmhouses (*fincas*), olive groves and unassuming old towns. The region is known as the 'Land of a thousand windmills' and, while it's unlikely anyone has counted, there certainly are a lot of them. They are a landmark of the island, and many have been restored and put back into use, particularly around Sa Pobla.

This route starts at Pollença and swings by several inland towns, with a detour to Randa, the 'monastery mountain', but narrow country roads shoot off in all directions and can be worth exploring.

Sa Pobla

The Ma-2200 runs about 12km (8 miles) through fertile farmland to **Sa Pobla**, an unexceptional but pleasant town with fine old buildings clustered around the main square and a church consecrated to Sant Antoni Abat. The Sunday-morning food market is worth a visit, and a jazz festival takes place throughout August.

From here, you can press on along the main Ma-13 to **Inca**. It is not a particularly interesting town but worth a visit for its *cellers* (see page 81) and for the factory shop selling Camper shoes.

Binissalem and Sineu

Binissalem, around 8km (5 miles) further down the main road, is the heart of the wine-producing district. Vineyards stretch for miles around – particularly attractive in late summer, when grapes are nearly ripe for picking. There's a wine festival here in September.

It's better, though, to take the rural (but good) road to **Sineu** ㉒, at the centre of

NOTES

On 16 January, a popular festival in honour of Sant Antoni Abat is celebrated in Sa Pobla, with an enormous bonfire, music and *espinagades* (pastries filled with spiced vegetables and S'Albufera eel). The next day, the town's more amenable pets are led in a street procession and then blessed outside the church.

the island, the pick of the inland towns. It has an elegant Gothic church, adorned with lovely reliefs by the Mannerist Gaspar Gener (1563–90), a Baroque retable and interesting modern stained glass. There are also a handful of attractive Renaissance mansions in the town, and a peaceful plaza with good restaurants. Its Wednesday-morning market is the most authentic on the island.

From Petra to the sanctuaries

From Sineu, it is about 11km (6 miles) to **Petra** ㉓. One reason people visit this sleepy little town is for the **Casa Museu Fray Junípera Serra** (www.fundacioncasaserra.org). Petra is the birthplace of Fray Serra (1713–84); one of Mallorca's best-known sons, he was a Franciscan monk who founded numerous missions in California and was canonized by Pope Francis in 2015 – no matter the devastating effects the missions (and European diseases) had on the Indigenous population. The museum, run by a dedicated Society of Friends, illustrates these and other New World missions; his house next door is more interesting, a modest place with cell-like rooms and a pretty garden. Wall tiles on the usually closed monastery of Sant Bernardino, opposite, depict the Californian missions; and signs lead to *Es Celler* (see page 81).

Colourful shutters in Sineu

CELLERS

Anyone interested in the true *cuina Mallorquina* – Mallorcan cooking – should visit a *celler*. These cool basement bodegas were originally wine shops and are still lined with huge oak barrels, but have now become restaurants, serving large helpings of island food. They exist all over the island, but there are some especially renowned ones in the inland towns. Inca has about half a dozen, of which *Can Amer* (www.celler-canamer.es) is the best known. In Sineu, the *Cellar Ca'n Font* on the main square is the place to go, while the best one in Petra is *Es Celler* (www.restaurantesceller.com). They won't suit anyone who wants to eat outside in the sun, but their cavernous depths offer cool respite on a hot day.

From Petra, it is less than 5km (3 miles) on the Ma-3320 to the main Palma road (MA-15). The first town en route in the direction of Palma is Vilafranca de Bonany, known for the production of sweet little tomatoes, garlic, red peppers and melons. A little further along, a turning on the right leads to **Els Calderers de Sant Joan** (www.elscalderers.com; charge), an eighteenth-century manor house with a chapel, granary and an extensive estate and farm. You can sample homemade products as part of the tour.

Still heading towards Palma, turn off at Algaida to visit **Puig de Randa**, the highest point on Es Pla at 543m (1781ft), crowned by the **Santuari de Nostra Senyora de Cura** ㉔ (www.santuaridecura.com), which has accommodation and a bar-restaurant. The philosopher and mystic Ramón Llull (1235–1316) established the original sanctuary. On your way up, you pass the Oratori de Gràcia and the hermitage of Sant Honorat. Randa is the centre of a little cluster of sanctuaries. Not far away, the **Ermita de la Pau** has a Romanesque chapel; and, just above the village of Porreres, you can drive the 4km (2.5 miles) up to the **Santuari de Monte-Sión**, which contains a fifteenth-century marble statue of the Verge de Monte-Sión.

To return to Palma, continue on the Ma-15 or divert onto the motorway (MA-19) at Llucmajor. For the east coast, take the Ma-15 towards Manacor, then north to Artà.

To the east

Highlights

- **Artà and Ses Païsses,** see page 82
- **Capdepera,** see page 84
- **Cala Ratjada,** see page 85
- **Cala Millor to Porto Cristo,** see page 86
- **Felanitx and the Santuari de Sant Salvador,** see page 87
- **Porto Colom to Cala Mondragó,** see page 88
- **Santanyí and Cala Figuera,** see page 89
- **Journey's End,** see page 90

Most of the bays and beaches along the east coast have become overdeveloped and overcrowded, but the resorts are nicer and far less excessive than those around the Bay of Palma, and some spots – harbours such as Port Colom and Cala Figuera – are still delightful. There are also two fortified towns in the northeast corner – Artà and Capdepera – and a string of amazing caves to visit, plus the prehistoric sites of Ses Païsses (near Artà) and Capocorp Vell, near the south coast.

Artà and Ses Païsses

Artà 25 lies 12km (8 miles) inland, a fortified town that has retained a friendly, everyday atmosphere, and not become a mere showcase for its historic sites. It has a handful of decent hotels with restaurants and is a good place to stay if you want to escape the crowded resorts of the coast.

In a palazzo on the Plaça d'Espanya, the **Museu Regional d'Artà** (temporarily closed at time of writing) rubs shoulders with the

Cruising off Cala Mesquida

town hall and has a series of archaeological finds dating from the Phoenician, Greek and Roman periods, as well as a natural science collection.

The ancient church of the **Sant Salvador**, with a large rose window above the main portal, is one of Artà's major sites. Beyond, the Via Crucis (Way of the Cross), a broad flight of steps flanked by cypress trees and stone crosses, leads to the **Santuari de Sant Salvador d'Artà**. Construction started in the thirteenth century on the remains of a Moorish structure and, today, you can walk along the walls of this shrine, providing splendid views across the plain to the coast. You may be lucky and arrive while a recital is being given in the church – a wonderful experience.

The prehistoric settlement of **Ses Païsses** ㉖ (charge) is about 2km (1 mile) southeast of Artà on the Cami Corballa. A path leads from the shady car park through an impressive gateway in the Cyclopean wall wrapping around the settlement. The ruins, concealed among holm oaks, include square foundations, a *talayot* (watchtower) with a small chamber at its base, and an oval chamber with the remains of several pillars.

Capdepera

Barely 8km (5 miles) east of Artà is the ochre-coloured town of **Capdepera**, its streets filled with flowers. Steps lead from the Plaça d'Espanya to the **Castell de Capdepera** (www.castellcapdepera.com; charge). One of the best-preserved castles in Mallorca, it originated in Roman times, was enlarged by the Moors and strengthened further by the Christians. Beneath the defensive wall, from which there is a superb view, crouches the nineteenth-century church of Sant Bartomeu.

View from Capdepera's castle

From Capdepera, a road cuts through farmland, past the Canyamel Golf Club (www.canyamelgolf.com), then winds high above the **Platja Canyamel** development to the **Coves d'Artà** 27 (www.cuevasdearta.com; charge). Carved out of the sheer cliff face, the caves are less commercialized than the Coves del Drac (see page 86), and the limestone rock formations

Cala Ratjada

are quite awesome. In the summer, you can hop on a boat here from Cala Ratjada.

Cala Ratjada

It is only 3km (2 miles) from Capdepera to **Cala Ratjada** (also spelled Rajada), a busy resort built on a grid pattern. It was once the most important fishing harbour on the island after Palma, but much of the port is now used for leisure, as you can see from the boats moored here. There is an abundance of accommodation, although much of it is prebooked by tour companies; and the rash of fast-food outlets and tourist-tat shops can detract from the atmosphere. However, much of the seafront is attractive, with restaurant tables set among pines and succulents. There is one sandy beach in the centre of town, where good waves attract surfboarders, but most people venture

NOTES

A unique way to see the island is from the air. Mallorca Balloons (www.mallorcaballoons.com; charge) offers several different flights, including trips over the Serra de Tramuntana mountains, moonlight experiences, breakfast flights and journeys to see the almond blossom in bloom.

to the beaches further north. The northernmost one, **Cala Agulla** is backed by beautiful, protected dunes.

The **Platja de Son Moll** to the south of the resort can be reached via the promenade. Still further south, **Sa Font de Sa Cala** is named after a freshwater spring that flows directly into the sea. Here, a lovely little beach has been completely overwhelmed by two huge hotel complexes.

On a hill above Cala Ratjada's harbour, the **Sa Torre Cega** can only be visited by prior reservation (www.fundacionbmarch.es), but the impressive modern sculpture displayed there makes it worth the effort.

Cala Millor to Porto Cristo

The next resort complex, **Cala Millor** is the largest and loudest on the east coast, where three separate *calas* merge together along the sandy beach of Son Severa. The resort is still growing, and the neighbouring promontory of **Punta de N'Amer**, a 200-hectare (495-acre) nature reserve, is the only area that has swerved development.

Taking the road south, you'll end up at **Porto Cristo**, an old-fashioned resort with a pleasant, local atmosphere. There is a large yacht marina, an unremarkable beach and a couple of traditional hotels vying with modern buildings. It's popular with Mallorcan visitors at weekends, when the narrow streets can get clogged.

Most of the tour buses here are ferrying visitors to the **Coves del Drac** 28 (www.cuevasdeldrach.com; charge), south of town. Seven daily tours in summer (four in winter) run through 2km (1 mile) of brightly lit chambers and spectacular formations, culminating with classical music recitals and boat trips on the 177m (581ft)-long subterranean lake named after Edouard-Alfred Martel, the French speleologist who explored the caves in 1896.

On the road to Manacor, the **Coves dels Hams** (www.cuevasdelshams.com; charge) are competing for subterranean custom by offering a digital 'virtual adventure'.

Felanitx and the Santuari de Sant Salvador

It's a pleasant drive south through agricultural land, with minor roads darting off to beaches. To the right, just before Porto Colom, is **Felanitx** – you will see watchtowers on the hill as you approach. This was the birthplace, in 1957, of the painter Miquel Barceló, and it is a good place to buy ceramics. There is a lively market on Sunday morning, and an impressive, partly thirteenth-century church, Sant Miquel.

En route to Felanitx, turn off to the **Santuari de Sant Salvador** ㉙, 509m (1670ft) above sea level. The first sanctuary here was built in 1348; today's structure dates from 1734. On one side of the hill is a 14m (46ft) stone cross, and on the other, the monument to Cristo Rei

Felanitx

(Christ the King). The monastery church contains a fine alabaster retable showing scenes from *The Last Supper*. There is also a display of championship cyclists' jerseys, fading in glass cases along with notes of homage to the virgin. You can drive right up to the sanctuary. There are magnificent views, and accommodation in the *Petit Hotel Hostatgería Sant Salvador* (www.cancalcohotels.com), with bright, airy rooms and a good restaurant.

Porto Colom to Cala Mondragó

Reached on the Ma-4010 from Felanitx, **Porto Colom** is still a working fishing port, where you can watch the daily catch brought ashore. There is a strip of beach along the bay, but the lack of a significant, sandy swathe has ensured that Porto Colom remains a pleasant place, with a pine-shaded promenade and some pretty, pastel-coloured houses. Holiday apartments line the streets inland, but the only real commercial development is around the bay at Cala Marçal, south of the harbour.

Cala d'Or is only 7km (4 miles) further south, but you have to swerve inland then return to the coast. A resort of many years standing, it has evolved into a huge, sometimes stylish complex taking in a necklace of coves and beaches. The architecture is homogeneous – low-rise, flat-roofed and often bright white. The bays are pretty, and the swimming is good; the harbour plays host to elegant yachts, and there are all the tourist facilities and watersports you could ask for.

If you want to escape it all, press on a little further south to **Porto Petro**, an attractive harbour with a yacht club and decent restaurants; then wend your way to **Cala Mondragó**, which is off the beaten track and practically undeveloped in comparison with most of the coast. It should stay that way, because the two miniscule sandy beaches are part of the 785-hectare (1940-acre) **Parc Natural Mondragó** 30 (free), which also encompasses farmland and wetlands. Walking tracks weave through the park, offering

Cala Mondragó

plentiful opportunities to birdwatch and look for the wild orchids growing beneath the trees. A couple of hotels and beach restaurants are here, but it's all very low-key.

Santanyí and Cala Figuera

Return to the main road and, after 5km (3 miles), you'll reach **Santanyí** ㉛, a mellow little town of honey-coloured sandstone with one gate, Sa Porta Murada, remaining from the fortified walls. The elongated Plaça Major is edged by friendly cafés, but is dominated by the huge fortified church of **Sant Andreu Apostol**, which has a famously ornate organ and incorporates the Gothic gems of the **Capella del Roser**, a survivor from the first church built on the site. There's an arty feel to Santanyí, with a gaggle of exhibition venues, and rows of antiques and ceramics shops.

Cala Figuera 32 is a delightful fishing port with neat green-and-white houses and a walkway flanked by boathouses right at the water's edge. A handful of leisure boats bob in the waters, but they do not outnumber or outshine the working vessels. There are plenty of restaurants and accommodation, but the tourist industry has not grown out of hand.

Journey's End

Back to the main road again, **Botanicactus** 33 (www.botanicactus salines.com; charge) is the first stop after Santanyí. This is one of the better botanical gardens in the Balearics, and contains 1500 different plant species. It's not all cacti – there's an artificial lake surrounded by palms, and an assortment of indigenous flowers.

Cala Figuera

Some 7km (4 miles) away, **Colònia de Sant Jordi** is one of Mallorca's earliest resorts. Its pleasant harbour is the starting point for trips to Cabrera, and you can walk around the dunes to the south of the bay. To the west of Sant Jordi, the sandy stretch of **Platja Es Trenc** is now a protected area, so major development will not be permitted.

The main road west from Santanyí, through a flat, agricultural landscape where many of the windmills have been renovated with brightly coloured sails,

CABRERA

Cabrera, an uninhabited island 17km (10 miles) south of Cap de Ses Salines, has been a nature reserve since 1991. In season, it's easily visited on a boat trip from Colònia de Sant Jordi (www.excursionsacabrera.es; charge), but otherwise – if you are travelling there independently – you will need permission to visit (www.reservasparquesnacionales.es). It is only 7km (4 miles) by 5km (3 miles) in size, with rocky coastline giving way to a rugged limestone interior, where a track leads 72m (236ft) up to the castle. There is a pair of dinky bays, good for swimming and snorkelling. Bring your own supplies, or opt for lunch on a tour boat, because there is nowhere to buy food or water. During the Napoleonic Wars, Cabrera was used to house French prisoners, and it was later garrisoned by the Spanish army.

leads to **Campos** ㉞, an agricultural town with two huge, sandstone churches. The Església Parroquial Sant Julià contains a painting by Murillo (1617–82), but it is usually only open for mass.

The road then heads to **Llucmajor**, an ancient town with a smattering of striking *Moderniste* buildings. If you want to drive straight to Palma, the motorway will take you almost the whole way. Otherwise, follow signs to **Capocorb Vell** ㉟ (www.talaiotscapocorbvell.com; charge), one of the better-known prehistoric sites in Mallorca. The foundations of 28 enormous buildings can be seen, and at the edge of the settlement are two massive *talayots* and three round towers.

You can drop down to **Cap Blanc** ㊱, where a lighthouse rises above a rocky promontory. From here, the road runs along a rather dull stretch of coast towards the **Platja de Palma**. **S'Arenal**, the largest resort, merges into **Les Meravelles** on a 7km (4-mile) strip of packed beaches, fast-food outlets, high-rise hotels, high-throttle clubs, English pubs, Murphy's bars and German beer halls. Approaching the yacht harbour of **Ca'n Pastilla**, the road becomes pedestrianized and more inviting – and then you are back in Palma.

Sailing around the island

Things to do

The diverse landscapes of Mallorca are a natural playground for outdoor adventures, but there is more to the island. The Balearic gem is rich with local culture, a vibrant art scene, lively nightlife and a thriving leather and glassware industry. More and more visitors are swapping coastal megaresorts for hiking and cycling through the mountains, birdwatching and experiencing the gastronomy.

Outdoor activities

Most outdoor activities in Mallorca revolve around the ocean and there is a huge range of things to do, from sailing, windsurfing and kitesurfing to stand-up paddleboarding, snorkelling and, of course, swimming. However, walking, climbing and birdwatching are catching up in popularity, drawing thousands of visitors to the island, especially in spring and autumn, when the mild weather makes hiking a pleasure, and numerous migratory species enthral birdwatchers. Mallorca is also a great place for cycling, horse riding and golf.

Sailing

The Balearics are a sailing paradise. British Olympic gold medallist sailor Sir Ben Ainslie is, for one, very partial to the archipelago. The island has a wealth of safe harbours and some 32 marinas, and thousands of foreign visitors moor boats here year-round.

You can **hire** various kinds of craft for an hour, a day or week at many beaches and hotels. The **Asociación Provincial de Empresarios de Actividades Marítimas de Baleares** is the biggest yacht charter company (www.apeam.com). The **Centro Náutico Port de Sóller** (www.nauticsoller.com) is a good bet for boat or kayak hire and organizes water-based excursions. The **Escuela Nacional de Vela Calanova** (www.portcalanova.com) offers intensive beginners' courses, while **Sail and Surf Pollença** (www.sailsurf.de) is a prestigious club that offers instruction for both early and advanced sailors.

Windsurfing is big in Mallorca

Windsurfing and waterskiing

There are windsurfing schools at several larger resorts. **Sail and Surf Pollença** provides windsurf hire and tuition, as does **Water Sports Mallorca** (www.watersportsmallorca.com), which has a school in Alcúdia offering windsurfing, kitesurfing, surfing and catamaran classes. Also in Alcúdia is Spain's longest cable ski for wakeboarders. On the east coast, windsurfing facilities are available at Cala Millor and Cala d'Or. Equipment can be hired on many beaches, including Cala Millor, Can Picafort and Port d'Alcúdia.

Scuba diving

Easily the best spot for scuba diving on Mallorca is the clear and reefy water in the southwest corner of the island, off Sant Elm. Here and elsewhere, scuba-diving equipment is available for hire if you have a qualification from your home country. The **Federación Balear de Actividades Subacuaticas** (www.fbdas.com) can give information and advice. The numerous scuba-diving clubs include two in the southwestern corner: **Dragonera Dives – Aqua Marine Diving** (www.aqua-mallorca-diving.com) and **Scuba Activa** (www.scuba-activa.com; temporarily closed at time of writing). There's also **Big Blue Diving**, in Palma Nova (www.bigbluediving.net), with numerous sites for people of all ability levels, and Scuba Mallorca in Port de Pollença (www.scubamallorca.com).

Boat trips

Boat trips are available from several points along the west coast. In Port de Sóller, **Barcos Azules** (www.barcoscalobra.com) runs a variety of tours around the rugged coast and tiny bays, including cruises to Sa Calobra. Trips operate from most ports, some using glass-bottomed boats.

Walking and climbing

The Mallorcan landscape is perfect for dedicated hikers and more leisurely walkers. April and May, when the island is carpeted in wildflowers, are the best months, while September and October are good, too. In the hotter seasons, start

Climbing is popular in Mallorca

early in the day or make use of the long evenings. Needless to say, correct footwear is essential, and common sense will tell you that a supply of water, a wide-brimmed hat and sunscreen are wise precautions.

The **Serra de Tramuntana** makes for the most dramatic scenery, for example, on the dramatic climb up to the Castell d'Alaró (see page 64) and between the Santuari de Lluc and the Cuber reservoir. In the southeast corner, a tangle of walking trails unfurls through the pine groves, marshlands and dunes of the **Parc Natural de Mondragó**. These are on flatter and more gentle paths than those in the northwest. The tourist office in Sóller produces a leaflet outlining walking excursions in the immediate vicinity. Maps are widely available in local bookshops and newsagents. In addition, the website www.camins-mallorca.info has lots of information. The best guided hikes are organized by the small, independent **Mallorca Hiking** (www.mallorcahiking.com).

Looking along the coast from Cap Formentor

There are also serious rocks in Mallorca for climbers. Contact the **Federació Balear de Muntanyisme** (www.fbmweb.com) for information and advice.

Golf

There are over twenty 18-hole golf courses in

Mallorca, and some are challenging enough for even the best players. You can also hire equipment and take lessons. The carefully landscaped **Arabella Golf** (www.arabellagolfmallorca.com) hosts a yearly 63-hole Golf Marathon, while the course at **Golf Santa Ponça** (www.golf-santaponsa.com) is one of Europe's longest. On the east side of the island, **Canyamel** (www.canyamelgolf.com) and **Capdepera** (www.golfcapdepera.com) are both popular. For further information, check the website of the **Federació Balear de Golf** (www.fbgolf.com).

Cycling: a popular pastime

Birdwatching

Mallorca is one of the most rewarding birdwatching sites in Europe. The island's resident birds are enticing enough, but it's the visiting species that generate most excitement. Migrant birds stop off in spring – as many as two hundred species have been spotted – and some stay for the summer. The best birdwatching sites are in the mountainous **Tramuntana** region, where rare black vultures and other birds of prey can be spotted; the **Parc Natural de Mondragó** for marine birds; and the **Parc Natural de S'Albufera** – probably the best wetland site on any Mediterranean island – for the widest variety of all. Head to the birdwatching centre in La Gola, Port de Pollença for further information.

Horse riding

There is a scattering of small ranches and stables across the island, and some *agroturisme* properties offer treks or can arrange them for you. A couple of reputable riding schools are **Ranxo Ses Roques** (www.ranxosesroques.com) and **Rancho Jaume** (www.ranchojaume.com).

Cycling

Bikes can be hired at most resorts. Check brakes and tyres, and make sure a lock and puncture kit are included. Ask at the local tourist office for information on cycling routes. In the capital, bikes can be hired by the hour or day at Palma on Bike, in the city centre

There are over twenty golf courses on Mallorca

(www.palmaonbike.com); the company also organizes guided tours. You can pick up e-bikes, road bikes and e-scooters here, too.

Tennis

It's unsurprising that tennis is a big deal on Mallorca when the island is the birthplace and home of tennis legend Rafael Nadal. His academy (www.rafanadalacademy.com), just outside his hometown of Manacor, has 26 courts and offers tennis camps for juniors and seniors, plus padel lessons. Big fans might want to stop by the Rafa Nadal Museum (www.rafanadalmuseum.com; charge) to learn more about the champion and his achievements and take part in interactive exhibits. There are smaller clubs and tennis training centres in Peguera and Santa Ponça in the southwest and Port de Pollença in the north.

Spectator sports

Football is as popular in Mallorca as in other parts of Spain, and there are dozens of amateur and semi-professional clubs. In 2016, American businessman Robert Sarver purchased **RCD Mallorca** (aka Real Mallorca) and, since then, the team has clawed its way back into La Liga and is now majority-owned by former professional tennis player Andy Kohlberg. They play at Son Moix stadium in Palma (www.rcdmallorca.es). Tickets are usually available on the day.

Mallorca plays host to a wealth of competitions and races throughout the year, and spectating is often as much a test of endurance as competing when temperatures soar. Try cheering along the runners in the Half Marathon Magaluf (www.halfmarathonmagaluf.com) or the cyclists competing in the Mallorca 312 race (www.mallorca312.com), both in April. There are also popular triathlon events in Alcúdia (www.ironman.com/races/im703-mallorca) in May and in Calvià (www.challenge-mallorca.com) in February.

Shopping in Pollença

Shopping

Shopping in Mallorca is more expensive than it used to be, but you will still find some bargains, particularly if you are looking for leather goods or glass. For designer labels, however, **Carrer Verí**, in Palma's old town, has some smart boutiques, as well as a clutch of antique shops; and **Carrer Estanc**, off the **Passeig de Born**, is lined with chic clothing and interior design shops. **Avinguda Jaume III** is the capital's major shopping artery, flanked by big-name clothing shops as well as a huge branch of Spain's biggest department store, **El Corte Inglés**, which has a supermarket in the basement.

Leather

The Balearic Islands are justly famous for their leather industries. Excellent shoes, belts and bags and some of the finest leather and suede jackets come from the archipelago. The focus of the industry is Inca, where you can shop at the factory outlets or the local market, though the goods may not be any cheaper than those you will find in Palma.

If you like shoes, then you'll love shopping in Mallorca. You can visit the factory shop of quirky **Camper** (www.camper.com) on the main road around Inca, whose highly individual shoes have become well known. Camper also has outlets in Palma, in Avinguda Jaume III and Carrer Sant Miquel. Less trendy, but extremely attractive and comfortable, are *abarcas*, the slipper-like sandals made in Menorca that have been worn by peasants for centuries.

Linen

Mallorca's embroidered table and bed linens are attractive, and the market in Llucmajor is a great place to find them. Other towns known for good-quality embroidery are Manacor, Pollença and Artà. In Palma, you will see shops selling fine, hand-embroidered linen – and many others churning out machine-made versions.

Glassware, pottery and wicker

High-quality **glassware** has been made on the island for centuries. The **Gordiola Museu del Vidre** (www.gordiola.com) factory and museum outside Algaida, on the Palma–Manacor road, is a good place to go. You can watch glass-blowing and browse the collection of antique pieces on which many current designs are based. It also has a showroom in Palma, at Carrer Victoria 2.

Pottery is another traditional craft. There are two main types of cooking pots: *ollas* (round) and *greixeras* (flat and shallow). **Siurells** are small, clay whistles painted in red and green, based on Phoenician and Carthaginian originals.

Wickerwork is also woven in the culture of the island, and a few artisan makers still craft baskets, bags, chairs and more. One of the most traditional and beautiful is the family-run Mimbrería Vidal shop in Palma (Carrer de la Corderia 13), run by the third generation of the Vidal family.

Food and drink

Mallorca is known for its herbal **liqueurs**, and the popular aperitif, **palo**, is a novelty. One of the biggest brands is Tunel; look for it in bright green bottles stamped with the train logo, and decide if you want the sweet variety (*dulce*) or the dry (*amargo*). Also worth trying is the orange liqueur, **angel d'or**, made in Sóller. Don't miss sampling the wine from Binissalem, as you're unlikely to find it outside the island. **Olive oil** from around Bunyola is an excellent buy, not cheap but fine quality. **Olives**, too, are worth taking home. For a selection of Mallorcan varieties, in all shapes, sizes and shades, acquire a plastic container and fill it up with a selection from the large tubs on market stalls. For specialized foodstuffs the most fascinating place is in the old-fashioned little **Colmado Santo Domingo** (www.colmadosantodomingo.com) in Palma on Carrer Sant Domingo, near the city tourist office. You'll spot it immediately as it's festooned with hams, sausages and strings of peppers and garlic. Remember to stock up on Flor de Sal from Salines Es Trenc for seasoning your dishes back home.

NOTES

An extraordinary treasure trove of new and second-hand English books can be found at **Fine Books** (www.instagram.com/englishfinebooks) in Palma: three floors of jumbled volumes, with everything from first editions to nearly new paperbacks, prints and old photos.

Markets

Weekly markets are held all over the island, where everything from fresh farm produce to leather bags, household linen, pots and pans, and sandals are for sale as well as a glut of replica clothing and bags. They usually start fairly early in the morning and

Olive selection

finish around 1pm. Particularly lively ones are held in Alcúdia on Tuesday and Sunday, in Pollença on Sunday and Sóller on Saturday. On Saturday morning in Palma, the **baratillo** (flea market) is worth a peek, even if you don't want to buy.

Culture

Music

Palma has a lively classical music scene. Two excellent concert halls, the Sala Magna and the Sala Mozart, are located in **Auditorium de Palma** (www.auditoriumpalma.com). The Ciutat de Palma Symphony Orchestra regularly performs here, and there is a varied programme of orchestral music, ballet, jazz and opera. The **Teatre Principal** (www.teatreprincipal.com) stages top-quality opera, classical recitals and jazz. In summer, concerts also take place in the music room of the **Palau March** (www.fundacionbmarch.es). Free outdoor performances – jazz, rock and classical – are held in the attractive setting of the **Parc de la Mar** beneath the city walls on some summer evenings. A bar serves drinks and snacks, and there's a party atmosphere.

Each June you'll find a host of live acts taking to the stage at the Mallorca Live Festival (www.mallorcalivefestival.com) in Magaluf. It's a three-day affair with lots of genres including rock, pop, electronic, and indie music.

Further around the coast, the upmarket marina of Port Adriano puts on another live music series (www.portadrianomusic.es) with

Summer music festival in Sant Joan

big-name headliners each year such as Tom Jones, Sister Sledge, Nile Rogers and Chic plus many other acts.

Art

The island is no stranger to artistic endeavours, having been home to many artists, painters and writers. There are many galleries and art museums in Mallorca, but a few standouts include the Fundació Pilar i Joan Miró (www.miromallorca.com), dedicated to the works of the famous artist, and the Es Baluard Museu d'Art Contemporani de Palma (www.esbaluard.org), with its three floors of modern and contemporary art. There's also a great roof terrace for taking in views of the capital and port. Don't forget to stop by the shop for artistic souvenirs.

Nightlife

The bars and clubs in the big resorts thump with loud music all night long and would be hard to miss. Needless to say, they rise and fall in favour, making it impossible to predict next season's hottest spot. They are mostly geared to the teen and early-twenties age groups, and there is no shortage of leaflets and posters trying to tempt customers.

Otherwise, most of Mallorca's nightlife is to be found in Palma, where the legendary club is **Social** (www.instagram.com/socialclubmallorca), which is due to reopen in 2025 in a brand-new location but will retain its cool vibe and discerning playlists. Remember that the action doesn't really start until around midnight. Elsewhere in the city, **Sala Luna** (www.lunapalma.es) always has a packed dancefloor, with echoes of neighbouring Ibiza.

Outside the clubs, much of Palma's nightlife takes place in late-night bars, many clustered in the Sa Llotja area, where most of the restaurants can also be found. The kitsch **Abaco** (www.bar-abaco.es), on Carrer Sant Joan (off Apuntadors), with its sultry decor, operatic background music and expensive cocktails, is an experience. For creative cocktails with a speakeasy style, head to **Chapeau** (www.instagram.com/chapeaupalma) or the elegant and innovative **Ginbo** (www.instagram.com/ginbobar). **Can Cuir** (instagram.com/cancuirlgbt) is a chic LGBTQ+ coffee shop by day and casual bar by evening often with entertainment.

Festivals and events

Summer is the time for music festivals, many held in beautiful historic buildings. The best-known one is the Deià International Music Festival (www.dimf.com). Most performances are in the stunning setting of Son Marroig. The Chopin Festival is held in the cloisters of La Cartuja in Valldemossa (www.festivalchopin.com), while the Festival de Pollença (www.festivalpollenca.com) attracts international musicians to the lovely cloister of Sant Domingo. There is a summer music event with performances in Palma's Castell de Bellver and in the Jardins Joan March Severa in Cala Ratjada (www.fundacionbmarch.es). Sa Pobla hosts an international jazz festival in August (www.sapobla.cat), while Palma stages music events in various venues as part of the Jazz Voyeur Festival (www.jazzvoyeurfestival.es).

Weekly street market in Santanyí

5–6 January: Three Kings (Reyes Magos) Procession in Palma.

Sant Antoni Abat festival

16–17 January: Sant Antoni Abat festival in Palma, Artà, Sa Pobla and Manacor; a procession of animals to be blessed by their patron saint.

19–20 January: Sant Sebastià celebrated in Palma and Pollença, where the *cavallets* (small papier-mâché horses that the dancers strap round their hips) perform in a procession.

February: Carnival (Carnaval) marked in many towns and villages with fancy dress parades and general revelry. This is a pre-Lent festival, so dates vary depending on Easter.

March–April: Semana Santa (Holy Week) is commemorated in Palma and throughout the islands with solemn processions, religious ceremonies and celebrations. In Pollença, the Devallament (Lowering) sees a figure of Christ brought down from the Oratori on the hill.

April: Half Marathon Magaluf through the streets of the coastal resort and Palma Nova. Mallorca 312 cycling race wends through the north, east and west of the island.

8–10 May: Cristianos i Moros festival, also called Ses Valentes Dones, in Sóller re-enacts a battle in 1561 when local women fought against invading Turkish pirates.

June: Mallorca Live Festival comes to Magaluf for three days, bringing a range of artists in different music genres.

13 June: Sant Antoni de Padua festival in Artà. Lively festivities involve *cavallets* and black demons that cavort around the streets.

15–16 July: Día del Verge del Carmen, the patron saint of fishermen and sailors, is celebrated in many ports across the island with

Holy Week procession, Llucmajor

processions on the water. Palma, Port de Sóller and Cala Ratjada are the principal venues.

Late July: Sant Jaume in Alcúdia is a big religious and secular festival, with parades and street parties.

24 August: Sant Bartomeu is celebrated in Capdepera and Montuïri with horse races and devil dancers.

28 August: Sant Agustí fiesta in Felanitx, with *cavallets* (carousels) and *cabezudos* (big papier-mache heads).

Cristianos i Moros festival

September: La Nit de l'Art transforms the capital into an open-air contemporary art museum as all the major galleries throw open their doors.

First Sunday in September: Processó de la Beatá in Santa Margalida.

Last Sunday in September or first in October: the Festa dies Butifarró in Sant Joan, with folk dancing and feasting on the famous Mallorcan black pudding (*butifarró*).

November: TaPalma food festival takes over the capital with world-renowned chefs and tapas competitions. The Festival of Light (also in February) occurs when the sun casts an image of the rose window in Palma Cathedral on the opposite wall.

31 December: Festa de Standa in Palma commemorating the Christian reconquest of the island under Jaume I in 1229, with a procession.

Food and drink

Restaurants in Mallorca cover a wide spectrum, from the excellent to the mediocre, from the local to the international. You'll find traditional, rural cooking – the hearty *cuina mallorquina* – as well as ubiquitous Spanish dishes like paella and gazpacho that are very popular, though they have little to do with the island. Over the past few years, there has a been a renewed emphasis on local produce and reimagining of classic dishes by Mallorcan chefs, many of whom have ventured to mainland Spain or further afield for their culinary training. As of 2025, there were ten restaurants with eleven Michelin stars, showing the elevation of the island's gastronomic scene, and while a meal in one of these restaurants is not cheap, it will generally be less expensive than it would be in many European capitals. Wine is also having a renaissance, with a surge of interest from locals and tourists alike in wines made on the islands using native grape varieties (see page 119).

Traditional Mallorcan tumbet

Top 10 things to try

1. Soups and stews

Soup might seem an odd thing to eat in a warm Mediterranean climate, but broths and soups are a mainstay of Mallorcan

Many restaurants spill outside onto the pavement

cuisine, particularly in winter. You'll most often find *sopas mallorquina* at *cellers* (rustic restaurants) in various forms, often combining vegetables, olives, garlic and sometimes pork. *Sopa* is usually served in an earthenware bowl, or *greixera de terra*, which in turn gives its name to a complete range of casseroles: *greixonera de peix* is a fish stew, and *greixonera d'alberginies* (or *berenjenas* in Castilian) is a wonderful aubergine concoction. Make sure to dunk the farmhouse bread you'll likely be served alongside the *sopa* in the broth.

2. Tumbet

You'll find *tumbet* on menus across the island and it can be served by itself or as an accompaniment to meat or fish dishes. It shouts Mediterranean as it's made of peppers, aubergine, tomatoes, olive oil, garlic and potatoes. It is similar to ratatouille in France and is a favourite vegetarian plate. It's an incredibly simple dish but packed with flavour and a common tapa.

3. Sobrasada

Every rural family on Mallorca once kept pigs, and many still do. Pork and its by-products are a mainstay, with local specialities including *butifarró* (a spicy sausage, either white or dark). But the Balearics are renowned for *sobrasada*, a spreadable chorizo pâté that takes centre stage on bread or crackers or makes its way into other dishes. It can be stirred into rices and stews or manipulated into inventive culinary creations like *croquetas*. One of the most common ways to see *sobrasada*, though, is grilled on toast and drizzled with local honey.

Sobrasada

4. Ensaïmadas

No Mallorcan breakfast is complete without one of these cloud-like swirls of pastry. The name derives from the word *saim*, meaning lard. Traditional *ensaïmadas* are dusted with icing sugar but you'll also find them filled with *crème pâtissière*, chocolate, *cabello de ángel* (literally 'angel's hair' but actually candied pumpkin). The most famous bakery for these sweet treats is *Horno Santo Cristo* (www.hornosantocristo.com),

BREAD AND OIL

Mallorca, whose landscape is dotted with ancient, gnarled olive trees and once-functional windmills, is renowned for its bread and oil – so much so that Tomás Graves, the son of Robert, wrote an entire book about it, *Bread & Oil: Majorcan Culture's Last Stand*. The bread is dense and biscuit coloured, the oil thick and rich and green. So, it is not surprising that *pa amb oli*, bread and oil (pronounced *pamboli*), is served everywhere. It is simply toasted bread rubbed with garlic, sprinkled with salt and drizzled with olive oil. As a refinement, it may also be flavoured with fresh tomatoes (*pa amb tomàquet*) and served with cheese, local ham, *sobrasada* or tuna. Cafés called *pambolierias* will present you with your chosen ingredients on a large platter, plus a bottle of olive oil, and leave you to assemble yourself a tasty, filling and budget-friendly snack.

which has been making *ensaïmadas* since 1910, and today has branches scattered across the island and even in the airport.

5. Coca

Another ubiquitous dish across the island, a *coca* is a type of flatbread often topped with different ingredients like a pizza (though the end result tastes quite different). The most typical version is *coca de trampó*, where the base is covered with a mix of vegetables, namely tomato, onion and peppers, drizzled with olive oil, sprinkled with salt and baked in the oven.

6. Arròs brut

Not to be confused with the Valencian dish of paella, *arròs brut* changes with the seasons but is essentially a rice dish with vegetables and meat (pork, chicken, rabbit). It's cooked with surplus broth, so it's not dry like paella. Tradionally, chicken or rabbit liver would likely have been added at the end for extra depth of flavour, as well as spices such as paprika and pepper for a punchy kick.

You'll find *arròs brut* at more classic restaurants such as *Mesón C'an Pedro* (www.canpedro.es) in Génova.

7. Llonguet

Every nation and food culture has some form of sandwich – and Mallorca is no different. A *llonguet* is a crusty bread roll typical of the island and very much a staple in Palma, so much so there is even a fair dedicated to the golden baps every April where more than 15,000 are sold. Anything goes when it comes to fillings: *sobrasada*, *jamón*, prawns, calamari, cheese and more. The *llonguet* is a bit of a symbol of the capital.

8. Fresh fish

Genuinely fresh fish and seafood are becoming something of a luxury in Mallorca. The seas have been overfished and local fishermen, in any case, could not keep up with demand in summer. If you ask, waiters will usually tell you honestly that much of the fish they serve is imported, frozen, from Spain's Atlantic ports. That said, there remains some wonderful just-landed catch to sample. *Salmonete* (red mullet) is caught locally, as are sardines *(sardinas)* and some of the *langostas*, spiny lobsters found on many menus. *Cap roig* – scorpion fish – is the choice Mallorcan fish; the cheeks are considered a great delicacy. Squid (*calamares*), cuttlefish (*sepia*) and octopus (*pulpo*), cooked in a variety of ways, are also widely available.

NOTES

There is also fruit, of course: sweet melons, juicy oranges, peaches and nectarines, fresh figs and grapes, all the better because they are locally grown and have ripened in the field, not in transit.

9. Flor de Sal

Sea salt has been harvested on the island for decades and is a great delicacy. It is prized by Mallorca's top chefs and mixologists who enhance their creations with the glistening crystals. You can learn more about the product at Salinas d'Es Trenc (www.flordesal.com) and pick up various types of salt in specialist shops such as in Mercat de l'Olivar (www.mercatolivar.com) in Palma.

Binissalem produces a good range of wines

10. Wine and spirits

There has been a steady production and promotion of wines from Mallorca over the past decade, and more bars and restaurants are stocking them. You'll often find home-grown labels paired with dishes on the tasting menus of top restaurants. Most come from the region around Binissalem, which lies between Palma and Inca. Many bodegas offer tours and tastings such as *Bodega Riba* (www.bodegaribas.com), the oldest winery on the island, which champions native grape varieties such as mantonegro. A local aperitif is *palo*, made from carobs and herbs and produced in Bunyola; and *àngel d'or*, made in Sóller, is a popular orange liqueur. The famous spirit Hierbas Túnel is often whipped out at the end of a meal in its iconic green bottle; be warned, it's delicious but potent.

Where to eat

While sitting by the water's edge might sound idyllic – and it is – don't miss out on venturing further inland for food and drink.

Can Joan de S'Aigo in Palma, Miró's favourite café

Cellers are the most typical Mallorcan restaurants and are often, as the name hints, underground like a wine cellar. They're a great way to escape the hot weather and keep cool while feasting on traditional cuisine. Look out for snails on the menu, which are a delicacy.

Elsewhere, bars, *tascas* and casual restaurants proliferate, particularly in resorts and in the capital. They mainly serve tapas and sharing plates, which you can mix and match and share among a group or simply sit up at the bar counter on a stool and perhaps order a local vermouth and a slice of tortilla.

More and more fine-dining and high-end restaurants are springing up as destinations in their own right, not just in Palma but across the island. For more rural offerings, look out for *agroturisme* properties where you often eat what's grown on site or nearby.

Eating habits

Local people eat late; lunch is between 1.30pm and 4pm, and any time before 9.30pm or 10pm is considered early for dinner. However, restaurateurs, aware that northern European visitors like to dine earlier, have adapted their opening hours accordingly. Remember that a restaurant that may look empty and unloved at 8pm might be packed out by 10pm.

As breakfast is insubstantial – coffee and toast or a croissant – lunch is often the main meal. Islanders generally have three courses, but it's perfectly acceptable to share a first course, or to order *un sólo plato* – just a main course. Many restaurants offer a *menú del día*, a daily set menu that's a real bargain; this is always available at lunchtime, and occasionally in the evening as well. For a fixed price, you get three courses – a starter, often soup or salad, a main dish and dessert, which is usually ice cream, a piece of fruit or a flan, plus bread, and a glass of wine, beer or bottled water.

In restaurants where locals are eating, you will notice that many of them order the *menú*, an indication that it is not one specially designed for tourists.

Reservations are necessary only at the more expensive restaurants or places that are popular for Sunday lunch.

Arroz brut, a hearty Mallorcan dish

To help you order

Could we have a table, please? **¿Nos puede dar una mesa, por favor?**

Do you have a set menu? **¿Tiene un menú del día?**

I would like... **Quisiera...**

The bill, please **La cuenta, por favor**

Deciphering the menu

agua water
vino wine
leche milk
cerveza beer
pan bread
entremeses hors-d'oeuvre
ensalada salad
tortilla omelette
pescado fish
mariscos shellfish
langosta lobster
calamares squid
mejillones mussels
anchoas anchovies
atún tuna
bacalao dried cod
cangrejo crab
pulpitos baby octopus
trucha trout
carne meat
cerdo/lomo pork
ternera veal
cordero lamb
buey/res beef
pollo chicken
conejo rabbit
poco hecho rare
al punto medium
bien hecho well done
asado roast
a la plancha grilled
al ajillo in garlic
picante spicy
salsa sauce
cocido stew
jamón Serrano cured ham
chorizo spicy sausage
morcilla black pudding
bocadillo sandwich
arroz rice
verduras vegetables
champiñones mushrooms
judías beans
espinacas spinach
cebollas onions
lentejas lentils
queso cheese
postre dessert
helado ice cream
azúcar sugar

Places to eat

Each restaurant and café reviewed in this Guide is accompanied by a price category, based on the cost of a three-course meal (or similar) for one, including a glass of house wine:

€€€€ = over €80

€€€ = €60–80

€€ = €40–60

€ = below €40

Palma

13% Carrer Sant Feliu 13a, www.13porciento.com. Just off Passeig des Born, this attractive wine bar serves excellent plates of local charcuterie as well as fish and meat courses, paired with a fine selection of wine by the glass or bottle. **€**

Bar Bosch Plaça Rei Joan Carles I 6, www.barbosch.shop. One of the most popular and inexpensive tapas bars in town, with a modest interior and a heaving pavement terrace. The traditional haunt of the city's intellectuals, and usually humming with conversation. **€**

La Bodeguilla Carrer Sant Jaume 3, www.la-bodeguilla.com. Slick and smooth establishment with softly illuminated lighting in the heart of the city, just off Plaça Rei Joan Carles I. The premises are divided into two – a small tapas and wine bar and a slightly larger restaurant (though tapas is served here too). It's the tapas you want, an exquisite range of Spanish/Catalan dishes – try, for example, the oxtail in a red wine sauce or the razor shell with roasted pickled tomatoes. **€€**

Can Cuir Plaça de la Quartera 9, www.instagram.com/cancuirlgbt. This LGBTQ+ café and bar is great for leisurely brunches or casual evening drinks, often with cultural and artistic events and live entertainment. **€€**

Ca'n Eduardo Carrer Contramoll Mollet s/n, www.caneduardo.com. On the top floor of an unassuming three-floor block beside the fishing harbour, this excellent restaurant surprises with a superb range of fish dishes. **€€€**

Celler Pagès Carrer Felip Bauza 2, off Carrer Estanc, www.cellerpages.com. Small and intimate *celler* with a family atmosphere serving traditional Mallorcan food – try the tongue with capers. Reservations advised. **€€**

Celler Sa Premsa Plaça Bisbe Berenguer de Palou 8, www.cellersapremsa.com. A local institution, with over sixty years under its belt. It pairs great ambience with a wide selection of classic, filling Mallorcan dishes. **€**

Forn de Sant Joan Carrer Sant Joan 4, www.forndesantjoan.com. Dining rooms spread across multiple floors, in the heart of the old town. A-la-carte Mediterranean dishes available, but it's essentially upmarket tapas – and very nice too. Also a good gourmet set menu. **€€**

Guethary Carrer de Marbella 36, www.guethary.es. A sublime and pared-back high-end restaurant among the rowdiness of Platja de Palma, *Guethary* is a breath of fresh air, inside *Iberostar Selection Playa de Palma*. Pick from a-la-carte or tasting menus, with optional wine pairings, to sample creative dishes showcasing the bounty of the sea. The exceptional fish and seafood dishes are prepared fresh on the open grill. **€€€€**

Marc Fosh Carrer de la Missió 7A, www.marcfosh.com. Epicurean dining at a Michelin-starred restaurant. An experimental menu draws on local produce from across the Balearic Islands, served in a relaxed ambience. Also offers wine tasting for oenophiles. Advance booking essential. **€€€€**

Mujer de Verde Carrer Sant Feliu 7, www.lamujerdeverde.com. Founded by the team behind Palma's oldest and best vegetarian restaurant, this vegan spot has a regularly updated menu, and its mouthwatering dishes mean the place is popular with carnivores too. **€**

Safrà 21 Carrer Illa de Corfú 21, Ciudad Jardin, www.safra21.com. At lunchtime, this restaurant specializes in traditional rice dishes whereas, come evening, it morphs into Mallorca's first 'bistronomic' restaurant, focusing on top-quality cuisine at reasonable prices. Out near the airport. **€€€**

The western corner

Banyalbufar

Son Tomás Carrer Baronia 17, www.facebook.com/restbarsontomas.banyalbufar. A small bar-restaurant whose terrace commands outstanding views of the coast. Fish comes directly from the boats in the cove; paella and the *arroz negro* (squid ink rice) are recommended. **€€**

Magaluf

El Chaval Carrer Violetes 2, www.elchavalmallorca.com. A casual but classy beachfront hangout at the end of the Magaluf promenade. Snag a table right at the water's edge and feast on fabulous grilled octopus, whole fish and a range of tapas, or simply pop by for a sundowner. **€€**

The west coast

Deià

El Barrigon Xelini Avinguda Arxiduc Lluís Salvador, www.xelinideia.com. Loud and lively place on the main village road specializing in tapas of all varieties. The stuffed squid is extremely good; the staff are friendly and casual. Grab a table on the outside terrace open in the summer. **€**

Sebastian Carrer Felipe Bauza 2, www.restaurantesebastian.com. Croquette of pulled pork with parsnip purée and a dollop of blueberry ketchup and rack of lamb with a honey-rosemary crust, green beans with bacon and potato purée are just two reasons to eat at this rustic but stylish restaurant, where the Mediterranean cuisine is front and centre. **€€€€**

Sóller

Bens d'Avall Urb Costa Deià, Carretera Sóller-Deià, km56, www.bensdavall.com. Situated around halfway between Sóller and Deià, this gourmet restaurant with an outdoor lovely terrace overlooking the sea specializes in New Balearic Cuisine made with local produce. **€€€€**

Sa Cova Plaça Constitució 7. Pleasant restaurant on the main square. Order the *conejo* (rabbit), a popular delicacy of the area. The seafood stew – *cazuela* – is worth the trip too. **€€**

The north

Alcúdia

Basico Steak House Carrer Serra 22, www.basicosteakhouse.com. Prettily located in the narrow streets of the old town, this popular restaurant, with its dinky courtyard and elongated windows, is the place to go for steak; barbecued steaks, to be exact. **€€€**

Cala Sant Vicenç

Lavanda Carrer Maressers 2, www.hotelcala.com. An excellent restaurant in the *Cala Sant Vicenç* hotel offering a refined Mediterranean menu paired with an excellent wine list. Set menu available. **€€€**

Pollença

Celler Es Molí Carrer Pare Vives 72. Well off the beaten track, in an ancient building on the corner of a narrow side street, this welcoming *celler* plates up authentic Mallorcan/Spanish cuisine at very affordable prices. The fish soup is especially tasty. **€€**

Port de Pollença

Bella Verde Vegan & Vegetarian Restaurant Carrer de les Monges 14, www.restaurantebellaverde.com. The only specialist vegan/vegetarian restaurant in this part of the island. Here, you can enjoy plant-based and meat-free dishes in the shadow of century-year-old fig trees. **€**

Stay Moll Nou s/n, www.stayrestaurant.com. A waterside spot in the centre of the port, the fittingly named *Stay* has been around for years. Fish is the first choice but there are meat dishes too, including lamb and pigeon ravioli. **€€**

The Central Plain

Inca

Joan Marc Plaça del Blanquer 10, www.joanmarcrestaurant.com. The locals' choice for the best restaurant in town, *Joan Marc* offers a chic but affordable take on classic Mallorquín dishes. **€€€**

Petra

Es Celler Carrer de l'Hospital 46, www.restaurantesceller.com. Huge and cavernous place serving up heaped plates of traditional food, including meat roasted in a wood oven. **€€**

Sineu

Celler de Ca'n Font Sa Plaça, www.canfontsineu.com. Another one of the traditional *cellers*, *Ca'n Font*, in a hotel of the same name, is the place to go for *sopas mallorquinas* (local soup), roast suckling pig and rice dishes. **€€**

The east and southeast

Artà

Finca Es Serral Cami Cala Torta, www.fincaesserral.com. Mallorcan and vegetarian cuisine in a rustic dining room or on the terrace of an attractive farm on the outskirts of town. **€**

Cala Figuera

Es Port Carrer Verge del Carmen 88. Eat inside or out, overlooking the bay. Spanish and Mallorcan specialities, fresh fish and signature pizzas. **€**

Cala Millor

Tapas de Sa Caleta Passeig Marítim 3, www.instagram.com/sacaleta calamillor. Great service and even better food. As the name suggests, tapas is the specialty. However, the menu is varied enough to cater to all tastes. **€€**

Porto Cristo

Vibes by Quince Carrer Bordils 51, www.restaurantevibes.com. You may be tempted to eat here just for the waterfront view, though *Vibes by Quince*'s popularity is as much about its excellent fish dishes as the vistas. **€€€**

Colònia de Sant Jordi

Salivent Carrer Cristòfol Colón, s/n, www.restaurantesalivent.com. Fabulous spot with views of the sea from the terrace, best taken in at sunset. Housed inside the *Iberostar Selection Es Trenc*, the restaurant takes its name from 'salt and wind'; fittingly, as the dishes made using local ingredients are imbued with Flor de Sal from the nearby salt plains. The rice dishes are superb. **€€€€**

Travel essentials

Practical information

Accessible travel

Palma airport and most modern hotels have wheelchair access and facilities for travellers with disabilities. There are also wheelchair-friendly buses. On the other hand, accessible public toilets are a rarity, few taxis are disability-friendly but can be booked in advance, and car-rental companies are, generally speaking, poorly stocked with adapted vehicles. Lots of resorts are well set up for those with additional mobility needs and many beaches have adapted access, some with amphibious chairs. Mobility Mallorca (www.mobilitymallorca.com) offers a wide range of mobility aids and scooters for hire.

Accommodation

Almost everywhere, hotel prices are governed by the season, with peak months (around June to August) costing much more than the shoulder and off-seasons; note, however, that many hotels in the resort areas close between November and March. In season, the majority of large resorts are block-booked by package tour operators. Breakfast is often, but not always, included in a room rate; check before booking. A value-added tax (IVA) of ten percent and the Sustainable Tourism Tax (€4, €3, €2 or €1 per night, depending on the type of accommodation; under-16s free) are added to the total; the latter is halved on the ninth day.

Accommodation ranges across a broad spectrum, although there are few pensions (guesthouses). *Hostales* (modest hotels) are graded from one to three stars, while *hoteles* (hotels) are rated from one to five stars. In recent years, there has been an ever-growing wave of boutique hotels on the scene, along with luxury resorts. Grades are more a reflection of facilities than quality: some two-star places can be superior to others with four. A new category – the *hotel d'interior* – has been introduced. These are small hotels (no more than eight rooms) that must be in traditional buildings, however minimalist their interior design may be.

Small hotels in rural settings and refurbished farmhouses and manor houses are called *finca* or *agroturisme*. They range from rustic to luxurious and many have minimum four- or seven-day stays. Rural Hotels Mallorca (www.ruralhotelsmallorca.com) has a particularly good range, albeit at the boutique end of the market.

All-in package deals can often be the cheapest option and provide a budget-friendly base for exploring the island. If you want to rent a villa or apartment, there are numerous agencies, including www.majorcanvillas.com and www.mallorca.co.uk. Finally, there is the opportunity to stay in a hilltop monastery or sanctuary, of which there are about eight; the most accessible is the Santuari de Lluc (www.lluc.net). The tourist office near the cathedral in Palma (see page 139) can provide a full list. These are fairly austere, but extremely economical and popular with locals and outdoor enthusiasts.

I would like a single/double room. **Quisiera una habitación sencilla/doble.**
With/without bathroom and toilet/shower **con/sin baño/ducha**
What's the rate per night? **¿Cuál es el precio por noche?**
Is breakfast included? **¿Está incluído el desayuno?**

Airport

Palma de Mallorca International Airport (PMI) is a sprawling affair located about 12km (7.5 miles) east of the city centre (www.aena.es/en/palma-de-mallorca.html). Taxis and buses link the airport with Palma; bus #1 leaves the airport every fifteen minutes from early morning until very late, running to Plaça d'Espanya (30min) and on to the port, with stops en route. There is a bus stop in front of the Arrivals Hall. Taxi is a little faster than the bus, taking around 15–20min, traffic permitting. They line up outside Arrivals; the approximate fare is €25.

Apps

There are a few useful apps you may wish to download for your visit, including EMT Palma, which provides timetables and bus stop locations around the city. Glovo is the go-to food-delivery app, with a range of restaurants serving most of the island. BiciPalma allows you to find rental bikes around the city, while Uber, Bolt and N Taxi all offer taxi rides.

Bicycle and scooter hire

A practical and enjoyable way to see the island is by bike, and you'll find rental outfits in most resorts – hotels and tourist offices have leaflets. Note, however, that you need to be very fit to tackle the steep roads of the Serra de Tramuntana mountains; cyclists are not allowed to use the island's main tunnel on the road between Palma and Sóller. Mopeds and scooters are also available, but you will need a special licence. Prices vary widely, so shop around. Remember that a helmet is compulsory when riding a motorbike, whatever the engine size. Ask for a helmet and for a pump and puncture kit, in case you get stuck with a flat tire miles from your hotel, and always carry ID. In Palma, try Palma on Bike (www.palmaonbike.com). Pro Cycle Hire (www.procyclehire.com), in Port de Pollença, will deliver your bike direct to your resort hotel if arranged in advance.

Budgeting for your trip

Mallorca once had a reputation for being cheap and cheerful, and while it's still possible to have an inexpensive holiday here – think monastery accommodation, for example – the island as a whole has moved upmarket. All prices below are approximate and given only as a guide.

Getting there. Air fares vary enormously. Flights from the UK with a budget airline can range from around £90 return off-season to £250 or more in high season. See www.skyscanner.net to compare prices.

Accommodation. Hotels can be more expensive than on the Spanish mainland. Rates for two sharing a double room during high season can start at €85 in a *hostal* to €400 at a top-of-the-range hotel. A comfortable, pleasant three-star will cost about €100–150. Rates drop considerably out of season.

Meals. The *menú del día*, a fixed-price midday meal, is usually an excellent bargain, costing around €20 for three courses, including a drink. In a bar, a continental breakfast (fresh orange juice, coffee, croissant) costs around €8; a coffee €3–€8. The average price of a three-course a-la-carte meal, including house wine, will nudge €40 per person. You can pay considerably less, but at top restaurants, expect to double that figure. The cost of wine has risen; a glass of wine in a smartish bar will set you back around €7.

Attractions. Most museums and galleries charge an entry fee of €3–5. Waterparks are more expensive, creeping up to €25 (children €18). A two-hour trip in a glass-bottomed boat costs around €20 (children half-price). You can usually find discounted and advance tickets online.

Ferries. Interisland ferries between Mallorca and Menorca are reasonable for foot passengers (about €50 return), but are more expensive if you take a car (between €100 and €300 for a vehicle and two passengers). The ferry from Mallorca to Ibiza is around the same price. Deals are often available, especially if you book well in advance. Note, however, that car-rental companies do not allow their vehicles to be taken from one island to another.

Car hire

Public transport is excellent, but if you do want to travel to every corner of the island, hiring a car is advisable. Major international companies – Avis, Hertz, Budget, Europcar – and Spanish national companies have offices at the airport and in Palma as well as in the major resorts. Many have weekly specials, which can work out as little as €30–40 a day. Rates are seasonal, and usually lower if booked online well in advance. Third-party insurance is included, but comprehensive insurance – *todo riesgo* – is usually extra. Be aware that policies may not cover off-road driving, and in-car satnavs often incur a hefty charge. In addition to value-added tax (IVA), an extra eco-tax of €3–7 a day is payable – the exact rate depends on the vehicle.

I'd like to rent a car. **Quisiera alquilar un coche.**
for one day/week **por un día/una semana**
Please include full insurance. **Haga el favor de incluir el seguro a todo riesgo.**

Drivers must be at least 18 or 21 (minimum age varies depending on car type) and have (generally) held a licence for at least six months. Hire companies will accept your national driver's licence. All of the below have an outlet at the airport:

Avis: www.avis.es
Europcar: www.europcar.com
Gold Car: www.goldcar.es
Hertz: www.hertz.es
Hiper: www.hiperrentacar.com

Climate

The sea is balmy for swimming from June to October. July and August can be scorching, and humidity may be high. Spring and autumn lure walkers and birdwatchers and those who enjoy sightseeing in cooler temperatures. Mallorca enjoys a mild winter, and many hotels stay open during the winter months. It can be chilly and wet at times, but a wall of mountains along the northwest coast protects the rest of the island from the worst of the weather.

The average temperatures below apply to Palma, but do not vary greatly throughout the islands, except in the mountainous areas.

	J	F	M	A	M	J	J	A	S	O	N	D
°C	10	11	12	14	17	22	24	24	22	18	14	12
°F	50	51	54	58	63	71	76	76	72	65	57	53

Crime and safety

Spain's crime rate has caught up with that of other European countries, and the Balearics is not immune, though they remain one of the safest places in Europe.

Be on your guard against purse-snatchers and pickpockets near Palma Cathedral and around the Plaça Major at night, and in markets and other crowded places. Take the same precautions as you would at home. In

Palma, report thefts and break-ins to the Policía Nacional; elsewhere, to the Guardia Civil. You need a police report for insurance purposes.

I want to report a theft. **Quiero denunciar un robo.**

Driving

Road conditions. There is a stretch of motorway around Palma and its bay, west towards Andratx, ending at Peguera, and east to Llucmajor. Another motorway runs north from Palma, via Inca, and continues behind the town to Alcúdia.

If you're driving from Sóller towards Palma, a tunnel carved through the mountains cuts the journey time. There's a good straight road running east–west across the island. Secondary roads are narrow but generally decent; on the mountainous northwest coast a series of hairpin bends tests the mettle of anxious drivers. Some of the mountain roads are nerve-jangling and best avoided after rain.

Rules and regulations. Drive on the right, overtake on the left. Seat belts are compulsory. Children under 12 must travel in the rear. Speed limits are 120km/h (75mph) on motorways, 100km/h (60mph) on two-lane highways, 90km/h (56mph) on other main roads, 50km/h (32mph), 30km/h (19mph) – or as marked – in densely populated areas.

Traffic police. Roads are patrolled (strictly) by the Guardia Civil de Tráfico, on motorcycles. Fines are payable on the spot. The permitted blood-alcohol level is low, and penalties are stiff.

Fuel. Service stations are plentiful. Petrol (*gasolina*) comes in 90 (super lead-free) and 98 (lead-free super plus) grades. Diesel fuel is widely available, too. Electric car-charging points are still thin on the ground, though they are increasing at a rate of knots.

Parking. Underground car parks have made life much easier for drivers in Palma (the one in Av. Antoni Maura by the cathedral as you enter town is a good one), while parking is less of a problem elsewhere. Most towns have metered areas, denoted by a 'P' and blue lines on the road.

Mechanical problems. Garages are efficient, but repairs may take time in busy areas. For emergencies, call 112. If you have broken down, call the emergency number provided by your car-hire company or, if it is your own vehicle, your insurance company.

Road signs. Most are standard pictographs; the phrases below may also be useful.

Aparcamiento Parking
Desviación Detour
Obras Road works
Peatones Pedestrians
Peligro Danger
Salida de camiones Truck exit
Senso único One way

Useful expressions:

¿Se puede aparcar aqui? Can I park here?
Ha habido un accidente. There has been an accident.

Electricity

Spanish **electricity** runs at 220 volts AC, with standard European-style, two-pin plugs. Brits will need a plug adaptor to connect their appliances; North Americans should bring both an adaptor and a transformer.

Embassies and consulates

The following are consulates:

UK: Carrer Convent dels Caputxins 4, Palma, tel: 933 666 200, www.gov.uk.

US: Carrer Porto Pi 8, Palma, tel: 971 403 707, https://es.usembassy.gov.

Ireland: Carrer Sant Miquel 68, Palma, tel: 971 719 244, https://www.dfa.ie/irish-embassy/Spain.

Australia, Canada, New Zealand and South Africa have no consulates in Mallorca; their nearest embassies are in Madrid.

Where is the British/American consulate? **¿Dónde está el consulado británico/americano?**

Emergencies

General emergency number (police, fire, ambulance): 112
National Police: 091
Municipal Police: 092
Guardia Civil (traffic): 062
Ambulance: 061
Fire: 080

Police! **Policía!**
Help! **Socorro!**
Fire! **Fuego!**
Stop! **Deténgase!**
Go away! **Váyase!**

Getting there

Air travel (see also Airports). Palma de Mallorca's airport is connected with London and most other UK cities by regular direct flights, as well as frequent services from many other European cities. For information on flights from the UK, check out the websites of Iberia (www.iberia.com) and British Airways (www.britishairways.com).

From Eire, the airline is Aer Lingus (www.aerlingus.com). Numerous budget airlines, including easyJet (www.easyJet.com), Flybe (www.flybe.com), Jet2 (www.jet2.com), Ryanair (www.ryanair.com) and Vueling (www.vueling.com), fly to Palma from airports all over the UK. Excellent bargains can be found for those willing to travel at very short notice, both for flight-only tickets and for package deals that include flights and accommodation.

By sea. Car ferries run daily from Barcelona and Valencia to Palma. The slower, overnight trip takes about eight hours to Palma on Trasmediterránea (www.trasmediterranea.es). Baleària has services from Barcelona to Palma (7hr 30min) and to Port d'Alcúdia (6hr 30min; www.balearia.com). It also provides a daily service from Dénia to Palma, which takes around 5hr 30min.

Guides and tours

Local tourist offices may have details of guided tours in the area, but here is a selection of the more interesting ones:

Mallorca Hiking: A wide range of guided walks – strenuous hikes, gastronomy, architecture – for all levels (www.mallorcahiking.com).

Mallorca Wine Tours: Trips around Mallorca's vineyards on a small tourist train (www.mallorcawinetours.com).

Palma City Sightseeing: Open-top bus tours of Palma (www.city-sightseeing-spain.com).

Tramuntana Tours: Walking, mountain biking and sea-kayaking in small groups (www.tramuntanatours.com).

Health and medical care

Standards of hygiene are generally high; the most common problems visitors encounter will be due to an excess of sun or alcohol. Tap water is perfectly safe, though many visitors stick resolutely to the bottled stuff. *Agua con gas* is carbonated, *agua sin gas* is still.

First-aid personnel (*practicantes*) make daily rounds of the larger resorts; some hotels have a nurse on duty. Many have medical centres (*centros medicos*), privately run institutions with English-speaking staff, where healthcare services must be paid for on the spot, in cash or by credit card.

Under reciprocal healthcare arrangements, citizens of the EU in possession of a **European Health Insurance Card (EHIC)** are entitled to free medical treatment within Spain's public healthcare system. Visitors from the UK are entitled to free, albeit limited, medical treatment under Spain's public healthcare system if they are in possession of a **Global Health Insurance Card (GHIC)**; if they previously had an EHIC, they can use this up until its expiry date.

Other non-EU nationals are not generally entitled to free treatment and should, therefore, take out their own medical insurance. That said, all travellers should consider private **health insurance** too, to cover the cost of treatment not covered within the EU/UK schemes, such as dental care and repatriation on medical grounds. No inoculations are currently required for Mallorca or Menorca.

Pharmacies (*farmácias*) are open during normal shopping hours, but there is at least one – the *farmácia de guardia* – open all night in Palma and in the large resorts. In small towns, it may be difficult to find an after-hours pharmacy. A list of the particular pharmacy on rota duty is (theoretically at least) posted in all chemists' windows.

Spanish pharmacists are highly trained and generally speak some English; they can dispense drugs over the counter that would often need a prescription elsewhere.

In Palma, the Farmácia March at Avinguda Joan Miró 186 (tel: 971 402 133) is open 24 hours a day, 365 days a year.

Emergency medical assistance can be obtained by dialling 112 or 061 (Ambulance).

Major hospitals located in Palma include Son Espases, on Carretera de Valldemossa, and Hospital de la Creu Roja Espanyola, at Carrer Pons i Gallarça 90.

Where's the nearest (all-night) chemist, please?
¿Dónde está la farmácia (de guardia) más cercana, por favour?
I need a doctor/dentist. **Necesito un médico/dentista.**
sunburn/sunstroke **quemadura del sol/una insolación**
an upset stomach **molestias de estómago**

Language

The Balearics, including Mallorca, has two official languages: Castilian Spanish – the national language of Spain – and Catalan, spoken here in the form of a local dialect, Mallorquín; almost all islanders speak both with equal fluency.

Street and road signs appear only in Catalan. English and German are widely understood, especially in the resort areas.

Do you speak English? **¿Habla usted inglés?**
I don't speak Spanish. **No hablo español.**

LGBTQ+ travellers

The Balearics are among the most hospitable places in Spain for LGBTQ+ travellers. Mallorca has a number of establishments, including hotels, bars, clubs and restaurants that cater for the LGBTQ+ community or are LGBTQ-friendly. For information on the best places, check out Ben Amics (www.benamics.com).

Money

Currency. Since 2002, Spain's currency has been the euro (€), which is divided into 100 cents. Bank notes are available in denominations of 5, 10, 20, 50, 100, 200 and 500 euros, and there are coins for 1 and 2 euros and for 1, 2, 5, 10, 20 and 50 cents. Note that the €500 is regarded with great suspicion – and many places will not accept them.

Currency exchange. You can exchange currency at banks (usually no commission charge) and *casas de cambio* (currency exchange stores), which stay open outside banking hours. Always take your passport as proof of identity. Check the rates carefully before handing over your money.

ATMs. The easiest way of obtaining cash but check how much your bank will charge you for doing so. Some credit-card companies don't charge for withdrawing money from ATMs abroad or for making other transactions; check in advance.

Where's the nearest bank/currency exchange office? **¿Dónde está el banco más cercano/la oficina de cambio más cercana?**
I want to change some dollars/pounds. **Quiero cambiar dólares/libres esterlina.**
Can I pay with this credit card? **¿Puedo pagar con esta tarjeta de crédito?**

Opening hours

Most shops and offices are open 9am–1pm and again 5–8pm. Many museums and other tourist attractions maintain the same schedule, although increasingly the more popular ones are staying open all day. Large supermarkets and department stores usually stay open all day and some until 10pm. Banks generally Mon–Fri 9am–2pm, and Sat 9am–1pm in winter only.

Restaurants serve lunch 1–3.30pm. In the evenings timing depends on the kind of customers they expect. Local people usually eat between 9.30 and 11pm. Places catering for foreigners may function from 7pm, and many serve food throughout the afternoon.

Police

Dial 092 for municipal police and 091 for national police. The general emergency number is 112. The municipal police station in Palma is located at Carrer de Son Dameto 1.

Public holidays

The following are official public holidays. There are a number of other holidays, usually saints' days, dotted throughout the year.

1 January **Año Nuevo** New Year's Day
6 January **Epifanía** Epiphany
20 January **San Sebastián** St Sebastian's Day
1 May **Día del Trabajo** Labour Day
15 August **Asunción** Assumption

12 October **Día de la Hispanidad** National Day
1 November **Todos los Santos** All Saints' Day
6 December **Día de la Constitución** Constitution Day
8 December **Inmaculada Concepción** Immaculate Conception
24 December Christmas Eve
25 December **Navidad** Christmas Day
26 December Boxing Day/St Stephen's Day
Movable dates:
Late March/April **Jueves Santo** Maundy Thursday
Late March/April **Viernes Santo** Good Friday
Late March/April **Lunes de Pascua** Easter Monday
Mid-June **Corpus Christi** Corpus Christi

Telephones

Spain's country code is 34. The local area code is 971 and must be dialled before all phone numbers, even for local calls.

Coin and card-operated telephone booths were once plentiful but are now all but obsolete.

To make an international call, dial 00, plus the country code and the phone number, omitting any initial zero.

If you are going to make lots of calls within Spain, it's worth buying a Spanish SIM card or new phone from a phone shop. Well-known networks are Movistar (www.movistar.es) and Vodafone (www.vodafone.es). If you're using your usual phone and SIM, check with your network provider before you travel that you have international roaming and find out if you can buy bundles of minutes to use abroad.

EU citizens can use their phones in other EU countries without incurring additional roaming fees: there is no extra charge for using your minutes, texts or data while you are away.

Time differences

The Balearics keep the same time as mainland Spain, which is one hour ahead of GMT, so Spanish time is generally one hour ahead of London, the same as Paris and Johannesburg, and six hours ahead of New York; it is nine hours behind Sydney and eleven hours behind Auckland.

Tipping

Tipping in Spain is not customary but, in some places, it is welcomed to leave something small. A service charge is sometimes included on restaurant bills (*servicio incluido*). If not, it is usual to tip waiters ten percent; you can leave a few coins, rounding up the bill, in a bar.

Give porters, hotel cleaners and hairdressers about €1–2. It is not expected to tip a taxi driver but for exceptional service, you can tip up to ten percent.

Toilets

There are many expressions for toilets in Spanish: *baños*, *servicios*, *lavabos*, *aseos*, *wc* and *bater*. The first three are the most common. Toilet doors usually have a 'C' for *Caballeros* (men), an 'S' for *Señoras* (women). Public toilets exist in some large towns, but they are rare; many bars will allow you to use their facilities.

Tourist information offices

Spanish National Tourist Office (SNTO). The compendious website compiled by the Spanish National Tourist Office (www.spain.info) provides an excellent introduction to the country; its myriad synopses – on everything from national parks to accommodation – are well written and succinct.

Tourist offices in Mallorca

Palma: For tourist information on the whole island, Plaça de la Reina 2. Municipal Tourist Offices (for information on Palma only): Plaça d'Espanya.

Sóller: Plaça d'Espanya.

Pollença: Carrer de Guillem Cifre de Colonya 4.

Transport

Mallorca has a reliable and comprehensive transport system, its buses and trains serving almost all the island's towns and villages. You can pick up bus and train timetables from the information office in Palma's Estació Intermodal (to the right of the entrance) or online at www.tib.org.

Bus. Buses (*autobús*) are clean, efficient and easy to use, and drivers are generally helpful. Destinations are marked on the front of the bus, and each town has its own bus station or terminal. In Palma, buses begin their journeys in the Estació Intermodal, the combined bus and railway station across the road from Plaça d'Espanya. Long-distance services are coordinated by Transports de les Illes Balears (www.tib.org), and Palma services by Empresa Municipal de Transports (www.emtpalma.cat). There is a set fare for city journeys, and you buy your ticket on the bus. There is also the hop-on, hop-off tourist bus.

Train. Mallorca has three narrow-gauge train (*tren*) lines. All of them depart and end at Palma's Estació Intermodal on Plaça d'Espanya. The first one runs from Palma to Inca, the second to Sa Pobla, the third Manacor. For more information, visit the Transports de le Illes Balears website: www.tib.org.

Ferries. Car ferries run a few times a day between Port d'Alcúdia and Ciutadella in Menorca, and take around two hours (Baleària, www.balearia.com). Transmediterránea (www.transmediterranea.es) has a weekly sailing from Palma to Mahón. Baleària also runs daily services from Palma to Ibiza, which take two hours. Note that you cannot take a hire car from one island to another.

Taxi. Taxi rates are metered and controlled by municipal diktat. In Palma, Radio Taxi: tel: 971 755 440; Taxi Palma Radio: tel: 971 401 414/971 702 424. In Sóller, tel: 971 638 484; Pollença, tel: 971 866 213; Cala Ratjada, tel: 971 819 090. Fares are reasonable, if not inexpensive: the cost of the 12km journey from the airport to the centre of Palma is, for example, €20; Søller to Pollença (55km) €90; there are small surcharges for excess baggage and late-night journeys. Always ask for a quote before you get in the car. A number of taxi apps are available (see Apps) including Uber.

How much is it to the centre of town? **¿Cuanto es para ir al centro?**

Visas and entry requirements

At time of writing, citizens of the EU/EEA, plus citizens of the UK, Australia, New Zealand, Canada and the USA, do not need a **visa** to enter Spain if staying for three months or less, but they do need a current **passport**. However, from late 2026, citizens from non-EU countries, including the UK, entering Mallorca for short stays will need an ETIAS (European Travel Information and Authorization System) – an online form, which must be completed before arrival and is an accompaniment to a passport. Visit https://travel-europe.europa.eu/etias_en for more information. Check before travelling as you will need to apply before you arrive in Spain. Travellers from South Africa currently need a passport and a tourist visa for visits of under three months; these must be obtained before departure and are available online from the Spanish embassy (see page 132).

For stays of **longer than three months**, there are few hindrances for EU/EEA residents, but everyone else needs a mix of **visas and permits**. In all cases, consult your Spanish embassy at home before departure. For UK citizens, updates are available on www.gov.uk.

Websites

www.illesbalears.travel Official tourist site for the Balearic Islands.

www.angloinfo.com/balearics Business directory, classifieds and what's on.

www.caminsdepedra.conselldemallorca.es Introduction to Mallorca's main long-distance hiking route, the *ruta de pedra en sec* (dry-stone route) – the GR221.

www.majorcadailybulletin.com Mallorca's leading English-language newspaper runs this offshoot website, offering a lively mix of news and gossip.

www.mallorca.es Outstanding government-run website covering every aspect of Mallorcan tourism.

www.spain.info Official website of the Spanish National Tourist Office (SNTO), providing an excellent overview of the country, with details on everything from national parks to accommodation.

www.tib.org Useful site carrying all the details of public-transport systems across Mallorca.

Index

M

N

O

P

R

S

T

V

MINI
MALLORCA

Second edition 2026

Editor: Joanna Reeves
Author: Phil Lee. **Updated** by Ross Clarke
Picture Editor: Piotr Kala
Picture Manager: Tom Smyth
Cartography Update: Katie Bennett
Layout: Claire Armstrong
Production Operations Manager: Katie Bennett
Publishing Technology Manager: Rebeka Davies
Head of Publishing: Sarah Clark
Photography Credits: Adobe Stock 104; Bar Cristal 16T; Bigstock 74; Fotolia 27; Glyn Genin/Apa Publications 115; Greg Gladman/Apa Publications 14BR, 15CB, 15CT, 24, 31, 37, 39, 40, 41, 42, 44, 45, 47, 48, 50, 55, 61, 65, 66, 68, 72, 76, 80, 83, 84, 89, 90, 94, 96, 100, 116; iStock 14CL, 14TL, 14BL, 15CT, 16CL, 62, 78, 92, 95, 103; Orient Express 16BR; Public domain 29; Shutterstock 1, 7, 8, 11, 12, 14TR, 14CL, 15T, 16CL, 18(all), 20(all), 23, 32, 34, 36, 46, 52, 54, 57, 58, 59, 63, 64, 69, 71, 75, 77, 85, 87, 97, 98, 106, 107, 110, 111, 112, 117
Cover Credits: Portocolom harbour **iStock**

About the author
Ross Clarke is an award-winning travel, food and wine writer. When he's not island-hopping the Canary or Balearic Islands or traversing mainland Spain in search of great stories, he's exploring the food, culture and history of his homeland of Wales.

Distribution
UK, Ireland and Europe: Apa Publications (UK) Ltd; mail@roughguides.com
United States and Canada: Two Rivers; ips@ingramcontent.com
Australia and New Zealand: Woodslane; info@woodslane.com.au
Worldwide: Apa Publications (UK) Ltd; mail@roughguides.com

Special Sales, Content Licensing and CoPublishing
Rough Guides can be purchased in bulk quantities at discounted prices. We can create special editions, personalized jackets and corporate imprints tailored to your needs.
mail@roughguides.com
roughguides.com

EU Representative
LOGOS EUROPE, 9 rue Nicolas Poussin, 17000, LA ROCHELLE, France; Contact@logoseurope.eu; +33 (0) 667937378

Printed by Omur in Turkey

ISBN: 9781835294093

This book was produced using **Typefi** automated publishing software.

A catalogue record for this book is available from the British Library

Contact us
Every effort has been made to ensure that this publication is accurate, free from safety risks, and provides accurate information. However, changes and errors are inevitable. The publisher is not responsible for any resulting loss, inconvenience, injury or safety concerns arising from the use of this book. If you notice any errors, outdated information, or potential safety risks, please send your comments with the subject line "Rough Guide Mini Mallorca Update" to mail@roughguides.com.